THE NEWEST GEORGE FOREMAN GRILL COOKBOOK 2023

1001 Days Delicious, Healthy, and Easy to Follow Recipes for Everyone Around the World

Brandon Gough

Copyright©2023 Brandon Gough
All rights reserved. No part of this book may be reproduced or used in any manner without the prior written permission of the copyright owner, except for the use of brief quotations in a book review.
First paperback edition May 2023.
Cover art by Natalie M. Kern
Printed by Amazon in the USA.

Disclaimer : Although the author and publisher have made every effort to ensure that the information in this book was correct at press time, the author and publisher do not assume and hereby disclaim any liability to any party for any loss, damage, or disruption caused by errors or omissions, whether such errors or omissions result from negligence, accident, or any other cause. this book is not intended as a substitute for the medical advice of physicians.

CONTENTS

INTRODUCTION 6

BEEF AND LAMB RECIPES 10

Meatball Marinara Sub 11
George Foreman Grill Cumin Lamb Steak 11
Fillet Steak Sandwich With Tomato Relish 12
Satay Beef Pitas 12
Beef Ramen Noodles 13
Asian Barbecue Beef Kabobs 13
Beef And Blue Cheese Sliders 14
Lamb Steak With Grilled Tomatoes And Potatoes .. 14
Grilled Lamb And Potato Salad With Peas And Mint 15
Tenderloin Steak | With Mushrooms & Blue Cheese 15
Cauliflower Steaks With Olive And Herb Salsa 16
Grilled Beef Fajitas 16

BREAKFAST RECIPES 17

Creme Egg Toastie 18
Triple Cheese And Cherry Tomato Pancakes 18
Homemade Granola 19
5-a-day Sandwich 19
Lamb Koftas With Flat Bread 20
Grilled Chicken Panini Sandwich With Pesto 21
Mac 'n' Cheese Toastie 22
George Foreman Grill Spring Onion Pancake 22
S'more Toastie 23
Grilled Pull Apart Bread 23
Breakfast Bap 24
Grilled Ribeye Steak Sandwiches 24
Banana Spice Waffles 25
Smoked Mackerel Sandwich 25
Big Omelette 26
Air Fryer Breakfast Flautas 26
Easy Breakfast Tacos 27
Wheat Pancakes 27
Brioche French Toast 28
Banana Bread Waffles 28

BURGERS RECIPES 29

Hellmann's X George Foreman Smash Burger 30
Mushroom Slinger Burger 30
Sweet Potato And Black Bean Burgers 31
Chilli Burger 31
New Zealand Lamb Burgers 32
Stacked Curried Burgers With Onion Bhaji 33
Welsh Lamb Burgers 34
Beetroot Burger 34
Halloumi Portabella "burger" 35
Curry Lamb Burger 36
Turkey Burger 37
Turkey Burger | With Grilled Fries 37
Black Bean Quinoa Burger Recipe 38
Turkey And Black Bean Burgers 38
Vegan Burger 39

DESSERTS RECIPES 40

Grilled Strawberry Maple Shortcake 41
Creme Egg Cookie Dough 41
Air Fryer Ramekin Cookie 42
Very Berry Cobbler 42

Banana And Fudge Pancakes 43	Pineapple Donut 47
Snickerdoodle Stuffed Croissant 43	Whipped Goat Cheese Polenta Waffles 47
George Foreman Grilled Peaches 44	Grilled Apple Cinnamon Skewers 48
Grilled Stone Fruit | With Rice Pudding 44	Grilled Pears | With Gingerbread Crumble 48
Grilled Pears | With Honeyed Yogurt 45	Chocolate Brownies 49
Peanut Butter Banana Panini 45	Lemon Poppy Seed Cake | With Plum Topping 49
Grilled Tiramisu Cake 46	Cookie Dough 50
Vanilla Fruit Kebabs 46	Grilled American Doughnuts 50

PORK RECIPES 51

Hot Sausage Sandwiches 52	Honey Bbq Pork | & Pineapple Skewers 54
Bacon Wrapped Stuffed Jalapeno Peppers & Yoghurt Dip 52	Cuban Pita 55
	Honey Mustard Pork Chops 55
Sweet Bbq Veggie Pulled 'pork' Quesadilla (vegetarian) 53	Greek Pork Chops 56
	Grilled Pork Cutlet With Rosemary 56
Brussels Sprouts With Chestnuts And Bacon 53	Bbq Pork Ribs 57
Apricot, Cranberry, Sage And Sausage Stuffing Balls 54	Apricot-glazed Pork Chops 57

FISH AND SEAFOOD RECIPES 58

George Foreman Grilled Catfish 59	Classic Crab Cakes 63
Lemon And Parsley Stuffed Grilled Trout 59	Lowfat Salmon Patties George Foreman Grill 63
Grilled Chilli Prawns With Lettuce And Polenta 60	Grilled Salmon On The George Foreman Grill 64
Cajun Shrimp 60	Fish Finger Sandwich 65
Honey Cumin Fish Tacos 61	Szechwan Tuna Steaks 65
Prawn Skewers 61	Grilled Tuna Salad Nicoise 66
Grilled Shrimp With Southwestern Black Bean Salad 62	Curried Fish Goujons 66

OTHER FAVORITE RECIPES 67

George Foreman Evolve Grill Pizza 68	Grilled Ham & Cheese Bagel 70
Bacon-wrapped Apps 68	Hoisin Duck Pancakes 71
Croque Monsieur 69	Cheats Calzone Pizza 71
Five Spice Duck 69	George Foreman Grilled Shishito Peppers 72
George Foreman Reheat Frozen Burritos 70	Lentil Dahl 72

POULTRY RECIPES 73

Grilled Greek Chicken Kabobs With Tzatziki Sauce 74	Air Fryer Homemade Chicken Tenders 75

George Foreman Grill Chicken Quesadillas............75	Chicken Quesadillas 81
George Foreman Grill Lemon Garlic Chicken 76	Buffalo Ranch Chicken Sliders...............................82
Lemon Tarragon Chicken With Grilled Zucchini And Potatoes..77	Piri Piri Chicken....................................82
	Creamy Cheesy Chicken Parcels............................83
Stuffed Chicken Breast 78	Korean Chicken Thighs 83
Best Damn George Foreman Grill Chicken Breasts.78	Yorkshire Pudding Wrap...84
Jerk Chicken Thighs 79	Chicken Wings.......................................84
Pesto And Parmesan Chicken Wings 79	Filipino Grilled Chicken 85
Parmesan Lemon Chicken Recipe..........................80	Chicken Kebabs 85
Turkey Meatballs 81	

SNACKS AND APPETIZERS RECIPES...86

Sweet Potato Hash Browns With Bacon 87	George Foreman Whole Roasted Brussel Sprout Stalk 92
Bbq Pulled Jackfruit 88	
Air Fryer Tortilla Chips 89	Mexican Bean Chilli..93
Roasted Pumpkin Salad 90	George Foreman Roasted Hatch Green Chile........94
Courgette Feta Fritters With Tzatziki 91	Easy Grilled Green Beans.......................................94

VEGETABLES RECIPES..95

Chilli Grilled Sweet Potato 96	Easy Foil Potatoes..102
Mexican Corn..96	Balsamic Grilled Beet Salad 103
Waffled Mashes Potatoes 97	Roasted Corn Salsa..104
Stuffed Mushrooms 98	Balsamic Carrots..105
Air Fryer Honey Garlic Cauliflower Bites 99	Grilled Stuffed Aubergine....................................106
Basic Grilled Crimini Mushrooms Recipe..............99	Spinach And Ricotta Lasagne..............................107
Grilled Broccoli For A Pan Or Outdoor Grill 100	Grilled Teriyaki Tofu 108
Vegan Chickpea Curry 101	

INTRODUCTION

Grilling can be intimidating, especially if you're new to it or have had some less-than-stellar results in the past. But with a little know-how, you'll be grilling like a pro in no time. Here are a few key things to keep in mind when using a George Foreman grill:

Cooking time: One of the great things about a George Foreman grill is that it cooks food quickly. However, it's still important to allow enough time for the food to cook fully. Different cuts of meat and types of food have different recommended grilling times, so be sure to do your research or use a meat thermometer to ensure your food is cooked to the desired internal temperature.

Cooking process: The George Foreman grill is a contact grill, meaning that the food is cooked on both sides at once. This can be a great time-saver, but it's important to pay attention to the cooking process to ensure that your food is cooked to perfection. For example, when grilling steak, it's a good idea to sear the meat over high heat first, then move it to a cooler part of the grill to finish cooking.

Simple steps: Grilling with a George Foreman grill doesn't have to be complicated. Simply marinate your meat in your favorite sauce or rub, and then just let the grill do the work. Keep it simple and let the natural flavors shine.

GRILL MAINTENANCE: KEEPING YOUR GEORGE FOREMAN GRILL IN TOP CONDITION

A well-maintained grill will not only last longer, but it will also give you better cooking results. Here are a few tips for keeping your George Foreman grill in top condition:

Drip tray: Many George Foreman grills come with a removable drip tray that catches excess fat and grease. Be sure to empty the drip tray after each use to prevent grease fires and to keep your grill clean.

Removable plates: Many George Foreman grills come with removable plates that can be taken out for cleaning. Be sure to remove and wash these regularly to keep your grill in good working order.

Nonstick cooking spray: Before grilling, be sure to coat your grilling surfaces with a thin layer of nonstick cooking spray. This will help prevent food from sticking and will make cleaning up a breeze.

Damp cloth: After grilling, use a damp cloth to wipe down the grilling surfaces. This will help remove any stuck-on food and will make it easier to clean the grill after it has cooled down.

SAFETY TIPS: USING YOUR GEORGE FOREMAN GRILL SAFELY

Grilling is a fun and enjoyable activity, but it's important to always be mindful of safety, especially when using electrical appliances like the George Foreman grill. Here are a few basic safety precautions to keep in mind:

Household use: Be sure to use your George Foreman grill only for its intended household use. Don't use it to burn trash or other materials, and always be sure to follow the manufacturer's instructions.

Electrical appliances: When using your George Foreman grill, be sure to use it only in a dry location and follow the manufacturer's instructions for proper use.

Electrical shock: To prevent electrical shock, be sure to unplug your George Foreman grill when not in use and never use it in the rain.

Indicator light: Many George Foreman grills have an indicator light that lets you know when the grill is on. Be sure to pay attention to this light and always turn off the grill when you're finished cooking.

INGREDIENTS AND TOOLS TO ELEVATE YOUR GRILL GAME

In addition to the right grill and good technique, there are a few key ingredients and tools that can help take your grilling to the next level. Here are a few ideas to get you started:

Olive oil: Use a high-quality olive oil to marinate your meats and vegetables for added flavor and moisture on your George Foreman grill.

Paper towels: Keep a roll of paper towels handy to clean up spills and wipe down the grill after use on your George Foreman grill.

Black pepper: Add a sprinkle of freshly ground black pepper to your grilled foods on your George Foreman grill for a boost of flavor.

Kosher salt: Use kosher salt to season your grilled foods on your George Foreman grill for a better flavor and texture.

Meat thermometer: A meat thermometer is an essential tool for grilling, and it's especially important when using a George Foreman grill. It will help you ensure that your food is cooked to the proper internal temperature, which is crucial for food safety. Always use a meat thermometer to check the internal temperature of your burgers to ensure they are cooked to the desired level of doneness on your George Foreman grill.

Soy sauce: Use soy sauce to marinate meats on your George Foreman grill for an added layer of flavor.

Vegetable oil: Use vegetable oil to coat your grill grates on your George Foreman grill to prevent food from sticking and to make cleaning up easier.

Liquid smoke: Add a few drops of liquid smoke to your marinade or rub to give your grilled foods a smoky flavor on your George Foreman grill.

I hope these tips and techniques will help you become a grilling pro with your George Foreman grill. Whether you're a seasoned grill master or just getting started, there's always something new to learn and try when it comes to grilling.

ELECTRIC GRILL VS. CHARCOAL: WHAT'S THE BEST WAY TO GRILL?

There are two main types of grills to choose from: electric grills and charcoal grills. Each has its own set of pros and cons, and the best choice for you will depend on your needs and preferences. Here are a few things to consider when deciding between an electric grill and a charcoal grill:

Electric grill: Electric grills are a great choice for those who want an easy, hassle-free grilling experience. They are often smaller and more portable than charcoal grills, and they are easy to use – just plug in, preheat, and start grilling. Many electric grills also come with features like temperature control and removable grilling plates, making them a versatile and convenient option. However, some people argue that electric grills don't provide the same level of smoky flavor as charcoal grills.

Charcoal grill: Charcoal grills are a classic choice for grilling enthusiasts. They tend to be larger and more expensive than electric grills, but they are known for their ability to add a smoky flavor to grilled foods. Charcoal grills also offer more control over the temperature, allowing for precise cooking. However, they can be messy to use and require more effort to set up and maintain.

Ultimately, the best way to grill will depend on your personal preferences and needs. If you want an easy, hassle-free grilling experience, an electric grill might be the way to go. But if you're a purist who craves that classic smoky flavor, a charcoal grill might be the better choice.

CONTACT GRILLS VS OUTDOOR GRILLS: WHAT'S THE DIFFERENCE?

Another choice that you have to make: contact grills and outdoor grills. While they may seem similar at first glance, they actually have some key differences that make them better suited for different situations. Here's a quick rundown of the main differences between contact grills and outdoor grills:

Contact grills: Contact grills, like the George Foreman grill, are designed to cook food on both sides at once. They have a top and bottom cooking surface that press down on the food, creating a "contact" between the food and the heat. Contact grills are usually smaller and more portable than outdoor grills, making them a great choice for small spaces or for those who don't have a lot of storage. However, they can't cook as much food at once as outdoor grills, and they may not provide the same level of smoky flavor.

Outdoor grills: Outdoor grills, also known as barbecue grills, are larger grills that are designed for outdoor use. They typically have a single cooking surface and use gas or charcoal as a fuel source. Outdoor grills are great for cooking large amounts of food at once and are known for their ability to add a smoky flavor to grilled foods. However, they can be more expensive and require more space and maintenance than contact grills.

GRILLING PLATES: WHAT ARE THEY AND HOW DO THEY AFFECT GRILLING?

Grilling plates, also known as grates, are the surface on which you place your food to grill. They come in a variety of materials and shapes, and they can have a big impact on the overall grilling experience. Here are a few things to consider when choosing grilling plates:

Material: Grilling plates are usually made of either metal or ceramic. Metal grilling plates, like stainless steel or cast iron, are durable and conduct heat well, making them a good choice for high-heat grilling. Ceramic grilling plates are a newer option that offers even heat distribution and is easier on the environment, but they may not be as durable as metal plates.

Shape: Grilling plates come in a variety of shapes, including flat, slanted, and waffle-patterned. Flat grilling plates are the most common and are good for grilling a variety of foods. Slanted grilling plates are great for draining excess fat away from the food, making them a good choice for healthier grilling. Waffle-patterned grilling plates are a fun option that add a unique texture to grilled foods, but they may not be as versatile as other shapes.

Size: Grilling plates also come in different sizes, and the size you choose will depend on the size of your grill and the amount of food you want to cook at once. Larger grilling plates will allow you to cook more food at once, but they may take longer to heat up.

Overall, the type of grilling plate you choose will depend on your personal preferences and needs. Consider the material, shape, and size when choosing grilling plates to get the best results for your grill.

GRILLING IN LESS TIME: TIPS AND TECHNIQUES FOR SPEEDING UP THE PROCESS

Grilling can be a time-consuming process, especially if you're cooking for a large group of people. But there are a few tricks and techniques you can use to speed up the grilling process and get delicious results in less time. Here are a few tips for grilling in less time:

Preheat your grill: One of the most important things you can do to speed up the grilling process is to preheat your grill. This will ensure that your grill is hot and ready to go when you start cooking, which will save you time and help you achieve better results.

Use thin cuts of meat: Thinner cuts of meat, like chicken breasts or pork tenderloin, will cook faster on the grill than thicker cuts like t-bone steak or pork chops. Using thin cuts of meat is a great way to reduce grilling time without sacrificing flavor.

Choose a non-stick grill: Grilling with a non-stick grill can save you time and hassle. Non-stick grills are easier to clean and are less likely to cause food to stick, which means you'll spend less time fussing with the grill and more time enjoying your meal.

Trim excess fat: Trimming excess fat from your meats before grilling can help reduce grilling time. Excess fat can cause flare-ups and can also cause your food to take longer to cook, so trimming it off will help speed up the process.

Grill in batches: If you're cooking for a large group of people, try grilling in batches rather than trying to cook everything at once. This will help you avoid overcrowding the grill, which can lead to uneven cooking and longer grilling times.

Overall, a little advance planning and the right techniques can go a long way in helping you grill up delicious meals in less time. With these tips and tricks in mind, you'll be able to enjoy all the benefits of grilling without spending hours over the hot coals.

THE BEST RESULTS WITH A GEORGE FOREMAN GRILL: TIPS AND TECHNIQUES

A George Foreman grill is a versatile and convenient appliance that can help you achieve great grilling results. However, like any appliance, it's important to use it properly to get the best results. Here are a few tips and techniques to help you achieve the best results with your George Foreman grill:

Follow the manufacturer's instructions: The first and most important step to getting the best results with your George Foreman grill is to follow the manufacturer's instructions. This includes things like preheating the grill, using the right cooking times and temperatures, and cleaning and maintaining the grill properly.

Use the right cooking times and temperatures: Different foods require different cooking times and temperatures to achieve the best results. Use a meat thermometer to ensure that your food is cooked to the proper internal temperature, and follow the manufacturer's recommendations for cooking times and temperatures.

Preheat the grill: Preheating your George Foreman grill is essential for achieving the best results. Preheating helps ensure that the grill is hot enough to cook your food properly and helps create those classic grill marks that everyone loves.

Use the right cooking oil: Using the right cooking oil can help prevent sticking and ensure that your food cooks evenly on your George Foreman grill. A high-quality olive oil or vegetable oil is a good choice for most grilling needs.

Clean and maintain your grill: Keeping your George Foreman grill clean and well-maintained is essential for getting the best results. Be sure to follow the manufacturer's instructions for cleaning and maintaining the grill, and be sure to clean the grilling plates after every use to prevent any build-up of food or grease.

Overall, following these tips and techniques will help you get the best results with your George Foreman grill. With a little bit of care and attention, you'll be able to grill up delicious meals that your friends and family will love.

BEEF AND LAMB RECIPES

Meatball Marinara Sub

 Servings: 6

Ingredients:

- 500g beef mince
- 1 white onion, finely diced
- 4 cloves garlic, finely chopped
- ½ bunch fresh flat leaf parsley, finely chopped
- 200g grated cheddar cheese
- 1 tsp cayenne pepper
- 1 tsp ground mace
- 1 tsp paprika
- Salt to taste
- 300-400g marinara sauce
- 200g grated mozzarella

Directions:

1. In a bowl, thoroughly mix together the beef mince, onion, garlic, parsley, cheddar cheese, cayenne pepper, mace, paprika, and salt.
2. Mould into 18 meatballs, then cover with cling film and refrigerate for at least 20 minutes. This will ensure the meatballs don't fall apart in the cooking process.
3. Pre-heat the Evolve Grill with the deep pan plate attached to the maximum temperature.
4. Cook the meatballs for 8-12 minutes with the lid down on your Evolve grill, turning occasionally to ensure they are cooked all over.
5. Add the marinara sauce to the deep pan, close the lid and bring to the boil.
6. Turn the grill down to medium and simmer for 10-12 minutes or until the meatballs are cooked through and the juices run clear.
7. Take the sub rolls and spoon 3 meatballs into each with some sauce. Sprinkle with the mozzarella and some parsley.
8. To serve: serve with mozzarella sticks and chips for the ultimate party meal.

George Foreman Grill Cumin Lamb Steak

 Servings: 2

Ingredients:

- 1/2 inch thick lamb steak
- Cumin
- Salt
- Pepper

Directions:

1. Preheat grill
2. Season lamb steak on both sides with salt, pepper, and cumin.
3. Grill for 5 minutes exactly without opening the grill.
4. Check it once at 5 minutes when it should be about medium rare. Total time depends on the size of the cut of lamb steak. Grill for longer to get to desired doneness.
5. When the lamb steak is done, put it on a plate and loosely cover with foil to rest for 3 minutes.
6. Wipe the grill down with a paper towel while it is still hot

Fillet Steak Sandwich With Tomato Relish

 Servings: 2   Cooking Time: 10 Mins.

Ingredients:

- 4 slices sour dough
- 2 tbsp olive oil
- 2 x 100-150g fillet steaks, lightly beaten
- Salt and pepper
- To serve:
- Tomato chutney
- Rocket leaves
- Sliced tomato
- Mayonnaise

Directions:

1. Pre-heat your George Foreman grill to maximum.
2. Brush the steaks with the olive oil and season with salt and pepper.
3. Once the grill is fully up to temperature, cook the steaks to your preference. The approximate timings are: 1½-2 minutes on each side for rare; 3 minutes on each side for medium; and about 4 minutes on each side for well done. If you're unsure, slice through the meat when you think it's done and if it needs more time, simply place it back onto the grill for a little while longer.
4. Once the steaks are cooked, set aside to rest.
5. To serve: Slice the sourdough into desired thickness, then smother with tomato chutney on one slice and mayo on the other, then layer on the rocket, tomato and steak, and dig in!

Satay Beef Pitas

 Servings: 4

Ingredients:

- 1tsp chilli flakes
- 2 garlic cloves, crushed
- 2tsp oil
- 350g steak, cubed
- 12 mushrooms
- lettuce leaves
- 4 whole wheat pitas
- Satay sauce
- 150ml coconut milk
- grated ginger
- 1 tbsp peanut butter
- 1 tsp fish sauce
- 1 tsp soy sauce

Directions:

1. In a bowl combine the chilli, garlic and oil. Add the cubed steak to the bowl, stir well to coat evenly then leave to marinade for 20 minutes.
2. Skewer the meat with the mushrooms and drizzle over any of the remaining oil.
3. Heat the grill to maximum temperature and grill for 4-6 minutes, depending on how you like your steak cooked.
4. Meanwhile, in a small saucepan, heat the satay sauce ingredients and bring to a simmer. Bubble, stirring occasionally until the sauce thickens.
5. Put the lettuce, meat and mushrooms into warmed pitas and pour on the satay sauce.

Notes:

1. If you're using wooden skewers, leave them to soak in water for an hour before using them so they don't char on the grill.

Beef Ramen Noodles

Servings: 4   **Cooking Time:** 20 Mins.

Ingredients:

- 2 x 250-300g rump steaks
- 2 tbsp. sesame oil
- 2 tsp. chilli paste
- For the stock:
- 300ml chicken stock
- 300ml beef stock
- 250ml water
- 3 tbsp. light soy sauce
- 3 cloves garlic, finely chopped
- ½ tsp. Chinese 5 spice
- ½ red chilli, finely diced
- 1 tsp. ginger puree
- To garnish:
- 350-400g cooked ramen noodles
- 4 soft boiled eggs, peeled and halved
- 8 baby sweetcorn, thickly sliced
- 100g baby spinach leaves
- 1 grated carrot
- 1 bunch coriander, chopped
- 2 spring onions, finely sliced
- 1 sheet dried nori, finely chopped
- Sesame seeds

Directions:

1. In a small bowl, mix together the sesame oil and chilli paste and brush over the rump steaks.
2. In a saucepan on the hob, combine the chicken stock, beef stock, water, light soy sauce, garlic, Chinese 5 spice, red chilli and ginger puree. Bring to the boil, then reduce the heat and simmer for 10-15 minutes. Strain the stock into a clean pan, and set aside.
3. Pre-heat your favourite George Foreman Grill to maximum. Cook the flavoured rump for approximately 3-5 minutes, then remove from the grill and rest for at least 5 minutes.
4. Add the baby sweetcorn to your strained broth and bring to the boil.
5. To serve: Divide the cooked noodles between 4 bowls. Divide the rump and baby spinach evenly and place on top of the noodles, then pour over the broth. Top with the boiled eggs, coriander, spring onions, nori and sesame seeds.
6. Dig in!

Asian Barbecue Beef Kabobs

Servings: 6

Ingredients:

- 3 Tbsp. Hoisin sauce
- ½ cup ketchup
- 1 green bell pepper, cut into 1-inch pieces
- ½ fresh, peeled and cored pineapple, cut into 1-inch pieces
- 1 ½ lbs. sirloin steak, cut into 1 ½ inch pieces

Directions:

1. Mix ketchup and Hoisin sauce in bowl. Add beef and toss until coated.
2. Preheat grill on setting #4 (medium high heat).
3. Arrange steak, pineapple and green pepper alternately on 6 (10-inch) wooden skewers.
4. Grill kabobs 10-15 minutes for medium doneness (160°F), turning once and brushing with extra sauce.
5. Serve with white or brown rice.

Beef And Blue Cheese Sliders

Servings: 8   **Cooking Time:** 3 Mins.

Ingredients:

- ¼ cup crumbled blue cheese
- 2 tablespoons green onion minced
- 1 teaspoon salt
- 1 teaspoon extra-virgin olive oil
- 1 pound extra-lean ground beef
- 8 small leaves of curly-lead green lettuce
- 8 slider buns or dinner rolls

Directions:

1. In a large bowl, mix together the blue cheese, onion, salt, pepper and oil. Add ground beef and lightly mix; do not over mix.
2. Divide the ground beef mixture into 8 equal portions and form into ½-inch thick patties.
3. Place the patties on a preheated George Foreman Grill and cook for 3 minutes, or until desired doneness.
4. Assemble each slider by placing 1 leaf of lettuce on the bottom half of each roll. Place a cooked beef patty onto the lettuce. Top each patty with the remaining half of the roll.

Lamb Steak With Grilled Tomatoes And Potatoes

Servings: 2   **Cooking Time:** 20 Mins.

Ingredients:

- 2x 250-300g lamb leg steaks
- 10-12 new potatoes
- 2 plum tomatoes
- Salt and pepper to taste
- Olive oil

Directions:

1. Cook the new potatoes in salted water until they start to go soft. Remove from heat, drain and run under cold water until completely cold. Then cut the potatoes in half and set aside.
2. Remove the stalk from the tomatoes and cut in half length ways.
3. Pre-heat your George Foreman Evolve Grill to medium, using the steak setting.
4. Brush the potatoes, tomatoes and lamb steaks with olive oil and season. Put the probe into the centre of the lamb steaks.
5. Grill the lamb steaks until the probe light turns green and the grill beeps (if you require the lamb steaks to be cooked more, set the grill to the well done setting). Remove the lamb steaks from the grill to rest.
6. Remove the probe from the grill and set the grill temperature to 220ºC. Grill the potatoes for 4-5 minutes then, add the tomatoes to grill with them for a further 2-3 minutes, or until charred and softened.
7. Serve with minted lamb gravy.

Grilled Lamb And Potato Salad With Peas And Mint

Servings: 2   **Cooking Time: 10 Mins.**

Ingredients:

- 1 lamb loin, trimmed
- 3 tbsp olive oil
- 6-8 new potatoes
- Salt and pepper to taste
- Store bought yoghurt and herb dressing
- To serve: Peas, rocket leaves

Directions:

1. Half each potato and boil in salted water until just cooked, for approximately 8-12 minutes, depending on the size of your potatoes.
2. In a separate pan, cook the frozen peas to the packet instructions then drain and set aside.
3. Once cooked, drain the potatoes fully and combine with 2tbsp olive oil and season to taste.
4. Pre-heat the grill to 220C. Grill the potatoes for 5-6 minutes until golden brown. Set aside.
5. Change the heat on the grill to the medium steak setting, then brush the lamb loin with the remaining oil, season and then insert the probe. Cook and then set aside to rest, then cut into chunks.
6. To serve: lay a handful of rocket on a serving plate, then add the lamb, cooked peas, and potatoes. Drizzle over the yoghurt dressing and dig in!

Tenderloin Steak | With Mushrooms & Blue Cheese

Servings: 4

Ingredients:

- 4 oz. sliced fresh mushrooms
- 1 strip bacon, cut into 4 pieces
- 2 beef tenderloin steaks, 4 oz. each
- ½ tsp. garlic salt
- ¼ tsp. coarsely ground pepper
- 4 tsp. crumbled blue or gorgonzola cheese

Directions:

1. Attach ceramic grill plates, and preheat grill to 375°
2. Place mushrooms on grill, top with bacon and grill 4 minutes
3. Remove mushrooms and bacon, set aside
4. Press SEAR button on grill, wait until it heats to 500°; season steaks with garlic salt and pepper
5. Place steaks on grill and sear for 90 seconds (grill will return to 350° after 90 seconds on sear)
6. Grill at 350° for 4 minutes
7. Remove steaks from grill and top with mushrooms, bacon, and blue cheese

Cauliflower Steaks With Olive And Herb Salsa

Servings: 4   **Cooking Time:** 10-15 Mins.

Ingredients:

- 2 cauliflowers
- 4 tbsp olive oil
- Salt and pepper to taste
- For the salsa:
- 60g green olives, finely diced
- 15g baby capers, finely chopped
- 1 lemon, juice and zest
- 3 tbsp. olive oil
- ½ bunch flat leaf parsley, chopped
- ½ bunch coriander, chopped
- Salt and pepper to taste

Directions:

1. Cut the cauliflower into approximately 2cm thick slices and brush evenly with 4tbsp of olive oil. Season with salt and pepper to taste.
2. Pre-heat your favourite George Foreman Grill to maximum – once up to temperature, grill the cauliflower steaks for approximately 6-12 minutes until cooked with the lid closed.
3. In a bowl, combine the chopped olives and capers, the lemon juice and zest, the remaining olive oil, parsley, coriander, and salt and pepper to taste. Mix well.
4. To serve: Spoon some of the salsa over each cauliflower steak and enjoy with your favourite sides.

Grilled Beef Fajitas

Servings: 4

Ingredients:

- 1/2 pound boneless beef sirloin steak, cut into thin bite-size strips
- 2 slices (1/2 inch thick) large onion, separated into rings
- 1/2 medium green bell pepper, cut into thin bite-size strips
- 2 tablespoons fajita seasoning
- 2 tablespoons lime juice
- 4 flour tortillas for burritos (8 inch)
- 4 tablespoons sour cream
- 4 tablespoons salsa

Directions:

1. Heat closed contact grill (George Foreman type grill) 5 minutes.
2. Meanwhile, in large nonmetal dish or resealable food-storage plastic bag, mix steak, onion, bell pepper and fajita seasoning; stir or turn bag to coat.
3. When grill is heated, place steak and vegetables on bottom grill surface, spreading evenly; close grill. Cook 4 to 6 minutes or until steak is desired doneness and vegetables are crisp-tender. Place steak and vegetables on plate; drizzle with lime juice.
4. Spoon steak and vegetables down center of each tortilla. Top each with sour cream and salsa. Bring sides of each tortilla up over filling; press to seal.
5. Clean grill by carefully wiping with damp paper towel. Place 2 filled tortillas on hot grill; close grill. Cook about 1 minute or until tortillas are heated. Repeat with remaining filled tortillas.

BREAKFAST RECIPES

Creme Egg Toastie

Servings: 2 **Cooking Time: 10 Mins.**

Ingredients:

- 4 slices brioche bread
- Spreadable butter
- 3 creme eggs

Directions:

1. Pre-heat your favourite George Foreman Grill to maximum.
2. Separately, cut each creme egg in half and spread butter on one side of each piece of bread.
3. Once your grill is fully heated, carefully lay two pieces of brioche on the grill plate, butter side down, and place three creme egg halves on each slice. Place the other pieces of brioche on top, butter side up, and close the grill lid.
4. Grill for 5-8 minutes or until the bread is golden and the creme eggs are melted and starting to come out of the sides of the bread.
5. Once cooked, remove from grill and let cool for a couple of minutes, then dig in and enjoy!

Triple Cheese And Cherry Tomato Pancakes

Servings: 4-6 **Cooking Time: 10 Mins.**

Ingredients:

- 150g plain flour
- 3 tsp baking powder
- ½ tsp salt
- ½ tsp cayenne pepper
- 60g parmesan cheese, finely grated
- 80g mature cheddar cheese, finely grated
- 1 small soft goats' cheese log, approximately ½cm dice
- 8-10 cherry tomatoes, cut into 8
- 2 sprigs flat leaf parsley, chopped
- 280ml milk
- 2 large free range eggs

Directions:

1. Sift the flour, baking powder, salt and cayenne. Separately combine the milk and egg yolks. Combine the 2 together and mix well.
2. Add the parmesan cheese, cheddar cheese, diced mozzarella, tomatoes and parsley and mix well.
3. Whisk the egg whites to stiff peak and fold into the mixture.
4. Pre heat the griddle side of your George Foreman Grill and Griddle, or alternatively a large greased frying pan. Spoon some of the mixture onto the griddle in even amounts and allow to cook for 1-3 minutes until the mixture starts to bubble. Flip over and cook for a further 1-3 minutes. Repeat until all mixture is cooked.

Homemade Granola

👪 Servings: 4

Ingredients:

- 1 Tbsp. honey
- 1 Tbsp. sunflower oil
- ½ tsp. vanilla extract
- ¼ cup flaked coconut
- ¼ cup raisins
- 1 cup rolled oats
- ¼ cup hulled sunflower seeds
- ¼ cup chopped pecans
- 1 tsp. cinnamon
- 2 tsp. brown sugar

Directions:

1. Mix first 6 ingredients in medium bowl. Add honey, oil and vanilla extract; mix well.
2. Attach griddle plate to Grill & Broil. Spoon granola mixture onto unheated griddle plate. Cook on LOW broil at 350°F for 10 minutes, stirring every 3 minutes.
3. Turn Grill & Broil OFF and let granola cool in griddle pan 30 to 45 minutes, stirring occasionally.
4. Place granola in medium bowl; stir in raisins.

Notes:
1. Enjoy this granola with milk for breakfast or layer it with yogurt and fresh fruit for a tasty parfait.

5-a-day Sandwich

👪 Servings: 1   🕐 Cooking Time: 5 Mins.

Ingredients:

- 2 slices of sourdough bread
- 2 sliced rounds of aubergine
- 2 button mushrooms, sliced
- 1/2 tomato, sliced
- Handful of spinach
- 1/2 avocado, thinly sliced
- Salt and pepper to taste

Directions:

1. Start by grilling the aubergine, mushrooms and tomato with the lid down for 3-5 minutes, or until they have nicely browned and are cooked to your liking.
2. Remove from the grill and add the sliced sourdough. Grill until nicely toasted, for about 2-3 minutes.
3. Assemble the sandwich with a layer of spinach on each piece of bread, then add the mushroom, tomato and aubergine to one side, and slice avocado to the other side. Add salt and pepper to each side to taste, and some chilli flakes if you desire. You can enjoy them as open loaded toasts at this stage or carefully press them together to make a delicious sandwich!

Lamb Koftas With Flat Bread

Servings: 6　　　**Cooking Time: 15 Mins.**

Ingredients:

- For the flat breads-
- 180ml water, luke warm
- 90ml Greek yoghurt, room temperature
- 30ml vegetable oil, room temperature
- 30g butter, melted
- 1 tbsp caster sugar
- 1 ½ tsp salt
- 450g strong white flour
- 5g yeast
- For the koftas-
- 600g minced lamb
- 2 tsp ground cumin
- 2 tsp ground coriander
- ½ white onion, finely diced
- 3 cloves garlic, finely chopped
- ½ bunch fresh mint, finely chopped
- 1 green pepper, finely diced
- ½ bunch fresh parsley, finely chopped
- Salt and pepper to taste
- 12 wooden kebab skewers

Directions:

1. In a bowl, mix together the yeast and water, then add the yoghurt, vegetable oil, and butter.
2. You can make the flat breads in a stand mixer if you have one, but you can make it by hand if not! In your bowl or mixer, add the yoghurt mixture and add the sugar and salt, and the sifted flour. Mix with a dough hook attachments or clean bare hands.
3. Remove from the bowl onto a floured work surface and using the heel of your hand, stretch the dough away from you and fold it back on top. Repeat this for 10-15 minutes until the dough starts to turn stretchy and elastic. Once kneaded, place in a bowl and cover with a damp tea towel, and leave in a warm place to prove for 1 hour and the dough has doubled in size.
4. Tip the dough onto a lightly floured surface and gently knock the air out of the dough. Cut the dough into 6 equal amounts and shape into balls. Place on a tray and cover and again leave in a warm place for 45 minutes to prove once more.
5. For the koftas, mix all of the remaining ingredients together and shape onto the skewers. Cover with cling film and refrigerate for at least 20 minutes.
6. Pre-heat your George Foreman Grill and Griddle to 3 on both sides, for the flatbreads take each ball and roll out to a size that fits on the griddle. Carefully place the rolled out dough on the griddle and cook for 4-6 minutes on each side, remove and repeat with all the dough. Place each kofta on the grill side and cook for 5-6 minutes, then move around and cook for a further 4-5 minutes until cooked through and the juices run clear.
7. Serve with tzatziki, hummus and salad.

Grilled Chicken Panini Sandwich With Pesto

 Servings: 2

Ingredients:

- 1 tablespoon unsalted butter, softened, more if desired
- 4 slices bread
- 1 tablespoon homemade or store-bought pesto, more for serving, if desired
- 2 slices cooked bacon
- 1 cup shredded rotisserie chicken, or 2 grilled chicken breasts
- 2 slices provolone cheese
- Steps to Make It
- Gather the ingredients. Heat a grill or panini maker according to manufacturer's

Directions:

1. Spread the butter on one side of each piece of bread.
2. Butter in bread
3. Flip 2 pieces of the bread over and spread 1/2 tablespoon pesto onto each.
4. Add pesto
5. Top the pesto with the bacon, chicken, and then cheese.
6. Top with cheese
7. Top with the remaining two bread slices, buttered sides up.
8. Cover
9. Place in the panini maker and cook for 4 to 6 minutes. If using a grill, cook the panini sandwiches until golden on one side, 2 to 3 minutes.
10. Put on grill
11. Then flip and grill the other side for another 2 to 3 minutes.
12. Grilled cheese
13. Cut the sandwiches in half. Serve immediately with extra pesto, if desired.
14. Grilled chicken panini sandwich on a plate

Notes:

1. Precooked bacon is available in the grocery store, but if you'd like to cook your own, you can fry, bake, or microwave the slices until crispy, and then drain on paper towels.
2. Almost any type of bread can be used in it, but make sure the slices are thick enough to handle the grill or panini maker. Heftier breads like baguette and ciabatta are great choices.
3. If you're so inclined, you can make homemade pesto and freeze the rest for later use.

Mac 'n' Cheese Toastie

Servings: 4   **Cooking Time:** 10 Mins.

Ingredients:

- For the toastie:
- 8 slices of thick white bread
- 2 tbsp. butter
- 4 pickled gherkins
- For the Mac 'n' Cheese:
- 40g plain flour
- 40g butter
- 450ml milk
- 50ml double cream
- 1/2 tsp English mustard
- 1/2 whole nutmeg, ground
- 200g grated mature cheddar cheese
- 500g macaroni, cooked in salt water
- Salt and pepper, to taste

Directions:

1. To make the cheese sauce, start by gently heating the milk on the hob, but do not fully boil. In a separate saucepan melt the butter, then add the flour to the butter once melted and cook for 1-2 minutes, stirring constantly. Slowly incorporate the heated milk a little bit at a time, stirring or whisking constantly, until all incorporated. This will become very thick to begin with but keep whisking and adding the milk slowly, and it will turn into a lovely creamy sauce. Once your sauce is made, season with salt, pepper and nutmeg, and stir through the mustard.
2. Remove from the heat and stir in the cheese and then the cream, then stir through the cooked macaroni. Pour out onto a large tray and leave to cool.
3. For the toastie:
4. Pre-heat George Foreman grill.
5. Butter one side of each slice of bread.
6. Sandwich your cooked Mac 'n' Cheese between 2 thick white slices of bread, butter facing outwards. Repeat until you have four sandwiches.
7. Place a sandwich onto the grill, butter side down, and grill for around 5 minutes or until the bread is toasted and the Mac 'n' Cheese is gooey and melted. Repeat for all sandwiches – if you are using a medium or large grill, you should be able to comfortably cook two at a time.
8. Once cooked, leave to cool for 5 minutes or so before serving, then tuck in and enjoy!

George Foreman Grill Spring Onion Pancake

Cooking Time: 7 Mins.

Ingredients:

- Frozen sheet spring onion pancake dough
- Oil

Directions:

1. Preheat the grill and brush or spray with oil
2. Place the frozen pancakes in a single layer on the grill
3. Grill for 7 minutes or until crispy and brown. If would like more crispy, add more oil to grill.

S'more Toastie

Servings: 2   **Cooking Time:** 10 Mins.

Ingredients:

- 4 slices brioche bread
- Nutella or other chocolate spread
- 10-12 marshmallows

Directions:

1. Pre-heat your favourite George Foreman Grill to maximum.
2. Separately, spread a generous layer of Nutella onto each slice of brioche.
3. Once your grill is fully heated, carefully lay two pieces of brioche on the grill plate, Nutella side up, and evenly dot your marshmallows on top. Place the other pieces of brioche on top to create a sandwich and close the grill lid.
4. Top tip: you may want to cut your marshmallows in half if they are extra big!
5. Grill for 4-6 minutes or until the bread is golden and the marshmallows are gooey and melted.
6. Once cooked, remove from grill and let cool for a couple of minutes, then dig in and enjoy!

Grilled Pull Apart Bread

Servings: 6

Ingredients:

- 1 French boule or sourdough loaf
- 3 Tbsp. butter, softened
- 2 cups shredded mozzarella
- 3 Tbsp. pesto

Directions:

1. Preheat the Indoor/Outdoor Grill on setting 5.
2. Cut the loaf on a diagonal into 2" diamonds, being careful not to cut all the way through the bread.
3. Using your fingers, open each crack and spread the butter and pesto onto the bread coating each piece completely.
4. Stuff the cheese into each crack.
5. Place a large piece of tinfoil under the bread and lightly wrap up the sides of the bread, leaving the top open.
6. Place the foil wrapped bread onto the preheated grill. Place the lid on the grill.
7. Grill the bread for 25-30 minutes, until the cheese is melted.
8. Serve as one large loaf and pull out chunks of bread to enjoy!

Breakfast Bap

Servings: 1   **Cooking Time:** 10 Mins.

Ingredients:

- 2 good quality sausages
- 3 rashers of smoked bacon
- 1 egg
- 1 brioche bun
- Optional:
- ketchup or brown sauce

Directions:

1. Pre-heat your George Foreman Grill and Griddle
2. Place your sausages on the grill and after 2 minutes add the bacon.
3. Crack egg onto the griddle for the remaining 6 minutes or until all food is piping hot.
4. Serve in a buttered burger bun topped with ketchup or brown sauce as desired.

Grilled Ribeye Steak Sandwiches

Servings: 4

Ingredients:

- FOR THE AIOLI:
- ¾ cup mayonnaise
- 1 Tbsp minced garlic
- Juice of ½ lemon
- 2 tsp Worcestershire sauce
- 2 tsp whole grain mustard
- 2 tsp horseradish sauce
- Salt and pepper to taste
- FOR THE SANDWICH:
- 2 Tbsp oil
- 1 large peeled and sliced yellow onion
- 1 each, seeded and sliced green and red bell pepper
- 1 pint sliced button mushrooms
- 2 tsp granulated garlic
- 4 10-ounce ribeye steaks
- 4 hoagie buns
- 4 slices Gouda cheese
- 4 slices provolone cheese
- Salt and pepper to taste
- OPTIONAL:
- Tomato
- Spinach
- Shaved Parmesan

Directions:

1. Preheat the grill.
2. For the aioli: Combine all ingredients in a bowl and mix. Refrigerate until ready to serve.
3. For the sandwich: Season both sides of the ribeye steak and set aside.
4. Put the oil, vegetables, garlic, salt, and pepper in a large storage bag, close the bag and shake to get the vegetables evenly coated with oil and spices.
5. Put some of the vegetables on the grill and close the lid. Cook until vegetables are soft. Take them off the grill and put them in a bowl. Set the bowl aside. Repeat as necessary until all the vegetables are cooked.
6. Take the steaks and put two at a time on the grill. Cook until the desired internal temperature is achieved. Set them on a cutting board and slice thinly. Repeat with the other two steaks.
7. Assemble the sandwiches: Divide the meat and vegetables between the hoagie buns and then place a slice of each cheese over the top of the vegetables and meat. You can put the sandwiches under a broiler or in a toaster oven to brown the cheese if desired. Tomato and spinach can be exchanged for mushrooms and peppers. Parmesan flakes can be exchanged for the Gouda and provolone.
8. Add the aioli and serve the sandwiches hot.

Banana Spice Waffles

Servings: 6

Ingredients:

- 2 bananas (blended to a purée)
- Waffle Mix (choose your favorite in-store mix)
- Ground cinnamon for dusting

Directions:

1. Create your waffle mix according to package instructions.
2. For 2-3 waffles, use ½ cup banana purée.
3. For 4-5 waffles, use ⅔ cup banana purée.
4. For 9-10 waffles, use entire banana purée.
5. Preheat George Foreman Grill & Broil to 400°F.
6. Pour ⅔ cup mix into each waffle plate section and close grill. Cook waffles for 5-6 minutes or until steam coming from waffles is minimal.
7. Sprinkle with ground cinnamon and serve immediately with maple syrup.

Smoked Mackerel Sandwich

Ingredients:

- 2 fillets of smoked mackerel
- 3 slices of wholemeal bread
- 4 cherry tomatoes, halved
- 1 bunch of watercress (aromatic plant)
- For the dressing:
- 2 tablespoons sour cream
- ½ teaspoon grated lemon zest
- ½ teaspoon lemon juice
- 1 teaspoon ground black pepper

Directions:

1. Prepare the dressing in a bowl and refrigerate for 2 hours.
2. Crumble the smoked mackerel on a slice of wholemeal bread, cover with the tomatoes and watercress, and then close with a slice of bread.
3. Grill for 2-3 minutes.
4. Add the dressing over the sandwich.

Big Omelette

Servings: 6-8　　**Cooking Time:** 15 Mins.

Ingredients:

- 6 large free range eggs
- 250g soft cream cheese
- 200g grated red Leicester cheese
- 2 mixed peppers, diced
- ½ red onion, finely diced
- 4 spring onions, finely sliced
- ½ bunch fresh chives, finely sliced
- Salt and pepper to taste

Directions:

1. In a bowl, mix together the eggs, cream cheese and seasoning.
2. Add in all of the other ingredients and mix well.
3. Pre-heat your George Foreman Evolve Grill to 175oC with the deep pan plate attached.
4. Carefully add the egg mixture to your deep pan plate and close the lid, and cook for approximately 12-17 minutes until cooked through and spongey.
5. Enjoy as a weekend brunch for the whole family!

Air Fryer Breakfast Flautas

Servings: 4

Ingredients:

- 1 Tbsp. butter
- 8 eggs, beaten
- ½ tsp. salt
- ¼ tsp. pepper
- 1 ½ tsp. cumin
- 1 tsp. chili powder
- 8 fajita size tortillas
- 4 oz cream cheese, softened
- 8 slices cooked bacon
- ½ cup shredded Mexican cheese
- ½ cup cotija cheese (or crumbled feta)
- AVOCADO CRÈME
- 2 small avocados
- ½ cup sour cream
- 1 lime, juiced
- ½ tsp. salt
- ¼ tsp. pepper

Directions:

1. In a large skillet, melt the butter over medium heat. Add the eggs and scramble until just cooked, about 3-4 minutes. Remove from heat and season with salt, pepper, cumin and chili powder.
2. Spread cream cheese down the center of each tortilla. Lay one piece of bacon on top of cream cheese and top with scrambled eggs and shredded cheese.
3. Tightly roll up tortillas.
4. Place baking rack in the bowl in the low position and place 4 tortillas, seam side down on top.
5. Tap the bake button and set temperature to 400°F and fry for 10-12 minutes, until tortillas are crispy.
6. Remove and repeat with remaining tortillas.
7. Meanwhile, add all avocado crème ingredients to a blender and blend on low-medium speed until smooth.
8. Spread avocado crème over flautas and top with cotija cheese.

Easy Breakfast Tacos

 Servings: 4

Ingredients:

- ¼ Cup cilantro
- 2 eggs, scrambled
- ⅓ Cup goat cheese crumbles
- 1 lime for slices
- salt and pepper to taste
- 1 scallion, finely chopped
- 1 Roma tomato, diced
- 4 tortillas

Directions:

1. In medium bowl, whisk eggs, salt and pepper.
2. Preheat Indoor/Outdoor Grill to setting 3.
3. Place whisked eggs on grill surface and grill until cooked or for approximately 4 to 5 minutes. Place tortillas on unused portion of grill to warm up. Remove tortillas from grill after 30 seconds.
4. Remove eggs from grill and evenly spread between four tortillas. Add diced Roma tomato, scallions and goat cheese.
5. Serve immediately with two lime slices per tacos to squeeze on top.

Wheat Pancakes

Servings: 2   Cooking Time: 10 Mins.

Ingredients:

- 180ml milk
- 1 lightly beaten egg
- 60g wholemeal flour
- 60g unbleached flour
- 1 Tbsp. sugar
- 1 tsp. baking powder
- ½ tsp. baking soda

Directions:

1. Pre-heat the griddle side of your George Foreman Grill and Griddle, or alternatively a large greased frying pan.
2. Mix dry ingredients in medium bowl. Add milk and egg, stir until combined.
3. For each pancake, pour a disk of batter on heated griddle. Cook 3 minutes.
4. Flip pancakes over and cook 1 minute or until pancakes are set and browned.
5. Remove pancakes from griddle and keep warm.
6. Repeat for remaining pancakes.

Notes:

1. To store leftover pancakes, cool completely and wrap tightly in plastic wrap. Store pancakes in the freezer up to one month. Defrost in refrigerator overnight before reheating.

Brioche French Toast

Servings: 8-10   **Cooking Time:** 10 Mins.

Ingredients:

- 6 large eggs
- 100g sugar
- 950ml milk
- 1 tsp ground cinnamon
- 1 teaspoon nutmeg
- 1 loaf day-old brioche bread, sliced 1" thick
- 2 tbsp butter
- Syrup, for serving

Directions:

1. In large bowl, whisk together eggs, sugar and milk. Add cinnamon and nutmeg; whisk to combine.
2. Layer bread slices in a shallow baking dish and pour over the egg mixture. Let the bread sit in the mixture for about 2 to 3 minutes to absorb the moisture and then flip over in the mixture for a further 2 to 3 minutes more to ensure the bread is fully coated.
3. Preheat your favourite George Foreman Grill.
4. Cook your slices of soaked bread on your grill until golden brown and crisp. Add small pieces of butter to the grill as necessary to help browning and to give French toast nutty flavour.
5. Transfer French toast to a baking sheet in a low heated oven to keep warm while grilling remaining slices. Repeat process with remaining butter and soaked bread.
6. Serve French toast immediately after dusting with icing sugar, top with syrup, and fresh fruit or bacon, if desired.

Banana Bread Waffles

Servings: 4

Ingredients:

- 1 tsp. baking powder
- 2 Tbsp. brown sugar
- ½ cup (1 stick) butter
- ½ tsp. cinnamon
- 1 egg, slightly beaten
- 1 cup flour
- ½ cup milk
- ½ tsp. salt
- ½ cup white sugar
- 1 tsp. vanilla
- 1 medium ripe banana, mashed

Directions:

1. Attach upper and lower waffle plates and preheat Grill & Broil to 400°F.
2. In large bowl, combine flour, baking powder, cinnamon and salt. Set aside.
3. In medium bowl, cream butter and brown sugar. Add in milk, egg and vanilla, mix until smooth. Fold in mashed bananas.
4. Pour wet ingredients into dry ingredients and mix lightly until combined.
5. Pour ⅔ cup batter on to preheated waffle plates. Cook 10-12 minutes, or until waffle is golden brown. Remove waffles and place on wire rack. Repeat with remaining batter.

Notes:

1. Serve warm topped with caramel sauce and chopped pecans.

BURGERS RECIPES

Hellmann's X George Foreman Smash Burger

⏰ Cooking Time: 15 Mins.

Ingredients:

- 450 g extra lean mince
- 4 Tbsp Hellmann's® Real Mayonnaise
- 2 cloves garlic, finely chopped
- 1/4 tsp ground black pepper
- 4 slices cheddar cheese
- 2 hamburger buns
- Lettuce, shredded
- Pickled gherkins, sliced
- Hellmann's® Chunky Burger Sauce

Directions:

1. Combine the mince, Hellmann's® Real Mayonnaise, garlic and black pepper in a bowl. Divide into 4 equal portions and roll into a ball.
2. Place the formed balls on your pre-heated grill and flatten them to your desired thickness.
3. Grill to your desired level, flipping the patties over to ensure even cooking.
4. Slice the burger buns in half and place them on the grill until golden brown.
5. Top each patty with a slice of cheese and close the lid of your grill until the cheese has melted.
6. Remove the buns and cover with Hellmann's® Chunky Burger Sauce.
7. Stack the bun with two of the cooked patties, topping with pickled gherkins, shredded lettuce and a final squeeze of Hellmann's® Chunky Burger Sauce.

Mushroom Slinger Burger

👥 Servings: 6   ⏰ Cooking Time: 10 Mins.

Ingredients:

- 650g beef
- 150g Portobello mushroom, finely chopped
- ½ white onion, finely diced
- 2 tbsp tomato ketchup
- 1 tbsp olive oil
- 2 cloves garlic, finely chopped
- 1 tsp English mustard
- 1 tsp horseradish sauce
- 1 tbsp Worcestershire sauce
- 80g breadcrumbs
- Salt and pepper to taste

Directions:

1. In a large bowl, mix together all of the ingredients, making sure to mix until fully combined and no pockets of breadcrumbs remain.
2. Divide the mixture into 6 equal amounts and mould into burger shapes. Transfer to a baking parchment lined plate or tray, cover and refrigerate for at least 20 minutes (or overnight if you're preparing ahead of time).
3. Pre-heat your favourite George Foreman Grill to maximum and cook the burger patties for 8-12 minutes until piping hot and the juices run clear.
4. Serve up with your favourite burger accompaniments – we've gone for a seeded white burger bun, a generous dollop of sweet tomato chutney, lettuce, American style cheese, tomato, and a drizzle of hot yellow mustard. Pair with a crispy side salad and some chunky oven chips for a Friday night dinner to be envied!

Sweet Potato And Black Bean Burgers

Servings: 4   **Cooking Time:** Mins.

Ingredients:

- 3 Sweet potatoes
- 1 tin Black Beans, drained
- 2 tbsp. Smooth peanut butter
- 4 cloves Garlic
- 1.5 tbsp. fresh minced Ginger
- 2 tsp. ground Cumin
- 1 tsp. smoked Spanish Paprika
- 1 tsp. ground Black pepper
- ½ tsp. ground Cardamom
- 1 Egg, beaten
- 1 tsp salt
- 1 tsp. Cayenne pepper
- 1 large Onion, finely chopped
- 1 Green pepper, finely diced
- 3 tbsp. porridge oats

Directions:

1. Peel and cook the sweet potatoes until tender and leave to cool.
2. Then place them in a food processor along with the peanut butter, garlic, half of the black beans and all the spices and blitz until smooth. Place the mixture in a bowl and add the rest of the beans, onions, green pepper, egg, and porridge oats. Stir well to combine. The mixture should be very thick and not too wet; if it seems wet, add a little more oats. It should seem like a "dough." Make 10 – 12 burger shapes.
3. Heat your George Foreman Grill and then place them in batches on the grill and cook for 5-6 minutes. The outer shell should be crispy but the centre will be soft and fluffy. You can eat these as they are or place them in a soft bun with a little lettuce.

Chilli Burger

Servings: 6   **Cooking Time:** 10 Mins.

Ingredients:

- 800g minced beef
- ½ red onion, finely diced
- 2 cloves garlic, finely chopped
- ½ tsp cayenne pepper
- 1 tsp chilli powder
- 1 tsp chilli flakes
- 1 tsp chilli paste
- 1 tbsp olive oil
- 2 tbsp tomato ketchup
- Salt to taste

Directions:

1. In a bowl, thoroughly mix all ingredients together.
2. Divide the mix into 6 equal amounts and mould into burger shapes.
3. Place onto a plate or two and cover with cling film. Refrigerate for at least 20 minutes so the burgers firm up before grilling.
4. Pre-heat your favourite George Foreman grill to its maximum temperature.
5. Cook the burgers for 8-12 minutes with the lid closed or until the juices run clear.
6. To serve, we recommend layering your burger patties in seeded burger buns with a slice of cheese, a generous dollop of sour cream and guacamole, and top with a tomato slice. For a real treat, top your burger with warmed leftover chilli con carne!

New Zealand Lamb Burgers

Ingredients:

- 6 Garlic cloves, chopped
- 1 tbsp. grated Lemon rind
- 1 tbsp. black Peppercorns (crushed)
- 800g Lamb Mince
- 200ml Olive oil
- 4 Shallots
- Salt
- Freshly ground Pepper
- 2 Bay leaves
- 2 red Peppers
- 80g light Muscavado Sugar
- 80ml Red wine vinegar
- 4 Burger buns
- 2 handfuls Rocket
- 5 tbsp. Hummus

Directions:

1. Firstly crush 4 garlic cloves, and add to the lamb mince along with the lemon rind and crushed peppercorns.
2. In a sauce pan place the chopped shallots and the other 2 garlic cloves (chopped), season and cook till soft. Add the bay leaves and chopped peppers and cook for a further five minutes. Add the sugar and vinegar and simmer to reduce liquid, about 30 minutes.
3. Meanwhile, heat your George Foreman and place the lamb burgers on the grill and cook for around 5 minutes or until it is cooked to your liking. When ready take off and place it under a sheet of foil to rest for around 5 minutes. This gives you enough time to slice your burger buns and place on the grill to toast for a couple of minutes and to soak up some of the amazing juices. Place a blob of hummus on each bun, add the rocket a lamb burger and finish with a good spoonful of the relish.

Stacked Curried Burgers With Onion Bhaji

Servings: 4   **Cooking Time:** 15 Mins.

Ingredients:

- 450g beef mince
- ½ red onion, finely diced
- 1 tsp curry powder, more can be added depending on your preference
- ½ tsp cumin powder
- 1 red chilli, seeds removed and finely diced, add to taste
- 1 green chilli, seeds removed and finely diced, add to taste
- ¼ bunch coriander, finely chopped
- Salt and pepper to taste
- For the onion bhaji:
- 1 large onion, finely sliced
- 60g gram flour
- 1 green chilli, seeds removed and finely diced, add to taste
- ½ tsp chilli powder
- ½ tsp turmeric powder
- Salt and pepper to taste
- Garnish:
- Tomato slices
- Lettuce leaves
- 4 x burger buns
- Mint riata
- Mango chutney

Directions:

1. For the burgers, combine all ingredients in a bowl and mix well. Divide the mixture into 4 equal amounts and mould into burger shapes. Refrigerate for at least 20 minutes.
2. For the bhaji, soak the sliced onion in water. In the meantime, combine all other bhaji ingredients together in a bowl.
3. Drain the onion then add to the combined bhaji ingredients and mix well. Divide the bhaji mixture into four equal amounts and mould into burger shapes.
4. For cooking, pre heat your Smokeless BBQ Grill to maximum temperature, using the temperature dial. Place the burgers on the grill along with the bhaji and cook for 4-6 minutes on each side making sure to cook the burgers through.
5. Before serving, we like to lightly toast the burger buns on the grill for 30 seconds to a minute.
6. Now it's time to assemble your burger! Start off with a spoon of mint riata onto the base bun. Next top with some lettuce and tomato, followed by your curried burger. Time to top it off with the bhaji on top, and a big spoon of mango chutney. Pop the top burger bun on, take a bite, and enjoy!

Welsh Lamb Burgers

Ingredients:

- Mayonnaise
- 1 Red onion, sliced
- 2 tsp. Balsamic vinegar
- 1 tsp. Olive oil
- 2 Tomatoes, Sliced
- 2 handfuls Rocket
- Salt and black pepper, to taste
- 8-12 Burger buns

Directions:

1. Firstly in a food processor blitz the garlic, rosemary, a twist of salt and pepper. Add to the lamb and along with the chopped mint mix everything well with your hands. Don't overwork the meat or you will toughen it.
2. Divide the mixture into 8 -12, then shape into slightly oval burgers.
3. Heat your George Foreman Grill and cook the burgers for 3 -4 minutes or until cooked.
4. For garnish take the sliced onions and tomatoes and toss them in the balsamic and oil with a twist of salt and pepper.
5. Take the French stick and slice it into burger sized pieces – place a burger, a spoon of the tomato and onion a few rocket leaves and top off with a blob of mayo

Beetroot Burger

Servings: 4   Cooking Time: 15 Mins.

Ingredients:

- 300g vegan mince
- 200g cooked beetroot, grated
- 200g chick peas, crushed
- 1 small white onion
- 3 cloves garlic, minced
- 4 tbsp olive oil
- 2 tsp chipotle sauce
- 60g breadcrumbs
- Salt and pepper to taste
- 4 burger buns

Directions:

1. In a large bowl, crush the chick peas with a fork or potato masher, then add in all of the rest of the ingredients, making sure to mix until fully combined.
2. Divide the mixture into 4 equal amounts and mould into burger shapes. Transfer to a baking parchment lined plate or tray, cover and refrigerate for at least 20 minutes (or overnight if you're preparing ahead of time).
3. Pre-heat your favourite George Foreman Grill to maximum. Brush the burgers with a little olive oil, season with salt and pepper, and cook for 5-10 minutes until slightly firm and crispy on the outside and piping hot in the middle.
4. Serve up with your favourite burger accompaniments – we've gone for a brioche bun, rocket leaves, a generous dollop of chipotle mayonnaise, tomato and thinly sliced shallot, grated carrot, thinly shaved cucumber, and avocado. Serve at your next BBQ or pair with a side salad and chunky chips for a real Friday night treat!

Halloumi Portabella "burger"

Servings: 6

Ingredients:

- PECAN KALE PESTO
- ½ cup pecan halves
- 1 cup loosely packed kale leaves
- 1 Tbsp. minced garlic
- 1 medium lemon, juiced
- 1 tsp. salt
- ¼ tsp. pepper
- ¼ cup grated Parmesan cheese
- ¼ cup olive oil

- "BURGER"
- 6 portabellinis (small portabella mushrooms), cleaned and dried
- 3 Tbsp. olive oil
- 1½ tsp. dried basil
- ¼ tsp. salt
- ⅛ tsp. pepper
- 8.82 oz. Halloumi cheese, sliced into 6 slices
- 6 ciabatta buns, sliced in half and toasted

Directions:

1. Preheat George Foreman grill by plugging it in, or setting it to MAX, 400°F or setting 4.
2. In bowl of a food processor, add all pesto ingredients except olive oil.
3. Process on low until thick paste starts to form.
4. With food processor still running, slowly pour olive oil through feed chute until kale has broken up into small pieces. Set aside. (Note: This will be chunkier pesto, and not as smooth as traditional basil pesto. It will also taste quite salty. The salt flavor will even out once on burger.)
5. In a small bowl, stir together olive oil from "burger" ingredients, dried basil, salt and pepper.
6. Place mushrooms on a cutting board and brush olive oil mixture over tops and bottoms of mushrooms.
7. Place mushrooms and halloumi cheese on preheated grill and close lid.
8. Grill mushrooms for 6 minutes, and cheese for 4 minutes.
9. Note: If grilling on Indoor/Outdoor grill, grill each for 4 minutes, flip and continue to cook for 2 additional minutes.
10. To assemble, spread pesto on the bottom of 6 toasted buns. Top with grilled mushroom and grilled halloumi cheese. Place remaining bun on top and eat immediately.

Curry Lamb Burger

Servings: 6 **Cooking Time:** 10 Mins.

Ingredients:

- For the burgers -
- 800g minced lamb
- 1 red onion, finely diced
- 2 tsp curry powder
- 1 tsp onion powder
- 1 tsp ground cumin
- 1 tsp ground coriander
- 3 cloves garlic, finely chopped
- 1 tsp ginger paste
- ½ tsp chilli flakes
- ½ bunch fresh coriander, chopped
- 2 tbsp olive oil
- Salt and pepper to taste
- To serve -
- 6 mini naan breads
- 1 tomato, diced
- ½ red onion onion, thinly sliced
- Small head of gem lettuce
- 6 onion bhajis
- Jar of mango chutney
- Raita or plain yoghurt

Directions:

1. In a bowl, combine all burger ingredients together and mix well. Divide into 6 equal amounts and mould into round burger patties. Cover with cling film and leave to rest in the fridge for about 30 minutes, or overnight if you need – this step is key to ensure the burgers hold their shape when being grilled.
2. Pre-heat your favourite George Foreman Grill to maximum. Cook the burgers until the juices run clear, which should take 8–12 minutes.
3. Plate up on top of a mini naan bread alongside some diced tomato, red onion, a lettuce leaf, and top with an onion bhaji, mango chutney and a spoonful of raita.

Turkey Burger

⏱ Cooking Time: 15 Mins.

Ingredients:

- 500g turkey mince
- 1 white onion, finely diced
- 1 tsp mustard
- ½ bunch fresh parsley
- Salt and pepper to taste
- 4 cheddar cheese slices
- 4 ciabatta buns
- Cajun mayonnaise
- 4 large lettuce leaves
- 1 avocado, crushed
- Half a small red onion, thinly sliced

Directions:

1. In a bowl, combine all burger ingredients together and mix well. Divide into 4 equal amounts and mould into round burger patties. Cover with cling film and leave to rest in the fridge for about 30 minutes, or overnight if you need.
2. Pre-heat your favourite George Foreman Grill to maximum. Grill the burgers until fully cooked and the juices run clear. If you are using an Evolve Grill, pre-heat the grill to 220°C with the probe set to 75°C. Insert the probe into the centre of one of the burgers. When the grill is ready, place the burgers onto the grill and cook until the probe light turns green and the grill beeps.
3. Remove cooked burgers from grill and place a slice of cheese on top of the patties while still hot, so the cheese melts.
4. Cut open ciabatta buns and grill slightly until lightly toasted.
5. To serve, spread some Cajun mayonnaise on the bottom of the toasted ciabatta, then place some lettuce on top. Place the cheesy turkey burger on top of the lettuce and top with some crushed avocado and sliced red onion. Finish with the top of the ciabatta buns and dig in!

Turkey Burger | With Grilled Fries

👥 Servings: 1

Ingredients:

- FOR THE FRIES:
- 1 small potato, cut into wedges
- 2 tsp. canola oil
- ⅛ tsp. salt & pepper
- FOR THE BURGER:
- 3 oz. lean ground turkey
- 1 oz. 2% cheddar cheese = ¼ cup
- 1 hamburger bun
- 1 cup vegetables of your choice: Tomato, onion, lettuce
- 2 Tbsp ketchup and/or mustard (optional)

Directions:

1. Preheat your George Foreman® grill.
2. Toss potato wedges in canola oil, salt and pepper and grill for 10 to 12 minutes. Set aside.
3. Form ground turkey into a patty and grill for 3 to 4 minutes.
4. As soon as you pull the burger off the grill, add the cheese. It will melt from the heat of the burger.
5. Assemble burger with bun, vegetables, and condiments and enjoy with grilled fries.

Black Bean Quinoa Burger Recipe

Servings: 8

Ingredients:

- ½ Cup cooked black beans
- 1 tsp. blackening seasoning
- 1 clove garlic, minced (2 tsp.)
- 1 small onion, finely chopped (1 Cup)
- 8 pretzel rolls
- 1 Cup quinoa
- ½ Cup fire-roasted stewed tomatoes, finely chopped

Directions:

1. Stir together quinoa and 1½ cups water in small saucepan, and season with salt, if desired. Bring to boil. Cover, reduce heat to medium-low, and simmer 20 minutes, or until all liquid is absorbed. (Makes 1½ cups cooked quinoa.)
2. Meanwhile, place onion and tomatoes in medium nonstick skillet, and cook over medium heat. (Oil left on tomatoes should be enough to sauté onion.) Cook 3 to 4 minutes or until onion has softened.
3. Stir in ½ cup black beans, garlic, blackening seasoning and 1½ cups water. Simmer 9 to 11 minutes or until most of liquid has evaporated.
4. Transfer bean-onion mixture to food processor, add ¾ cup cooked quinoa, and process until smooth. Transfer to bowl and stir in remaining ¾ cup quinoa. Season with salt and pepper, if desired, and cool.
5. Preheat Indoor/Outdoor Grill on setting 4. Shape bean mixture into 8 patties (½ cup each), and place on grill. Grill for about 8 to 10 minutes or 4 to 5 minutes per side.
6. Serve on pretzel rolls with your standard burger condiments.

Turkey And Black Bean Burgers

Servings: 6 **Cooking Time: 10 Mins.**

Ingredients:

- 750g turkey mince
- 1 x 400g tin black beans, drained and lightly crushed
- 1 red onion, finely diced
- 2 cloves garlic, finely chopped
- 1 red pepper, deseeded and finely diced
- ½ tsp ground cumin
- ½ tsp paprika
- Salt and pepper to taste

Directions:

1. In a large bowl, lighty crush the drained black beans with a fork or potato masher - you want these to remain quite chunky so do not over mash! Add all of the rest of the ingredients and mix well.
2. Divide the mixture into 6 equal amounts and mould into burger patty shapes.
3. Pre-heat your favourite George Foreman Grill to maximum. Lightly brush the burgers with olive oil and grill for 6-12 minutes with the lid down - if using the Smokeless BBQ Grill, be sure to flip the burgers half way through and add on an extra minute or two. Make sure to grill until the burgers are cooked through and the juices run clear.
4. Serve with your favourite burger accompaniments and sides - we recommend a fresh sesame seed burger bun, with a generous helping of cajun mayonnaise, then some lettuce, tomato and sliced avocado, and paired with sweet potato fries!

Vegan Burger

Servings: 6 **Cooking Time: 10 Mins.**

Ingredients:

- 400g green lentils, cooked, drained and slightly crushed
- 100g chickpeas, cooked, drained and slightly crushed
- 80g carrot, finely grated
- 100g celeriac, finely grated
- 80g onion, finely chopped
- 4 garlic cloves, finely chopped
- 2 tbsp. thyme leaves
- 2 sprigs Thyme
- 4 tbsp. olive oil
- 160g roasted butternut squash, slightly crushed
- 2 tsp chilli flakes
- 1 tsp smoked paprika
- 1 ½ tsp ground mace
- 2 tsp Cajun spice
- 180g fine breadcrumbs
- Salt and cracked black pepper to taste
- 6 burger baps
- Optional: Sriracha mayo

Directions:

1. In a bowl, combine all burger ingredients together and mix well. Divide into 6 equal amounts and mould into round burger patties. Cover with cling film and leave to rest in the fridge for about 30 minutes, or overnight if you need.
2. Pre-heat your favourite George Foreman Grill to maximum. Grill the burgers until fully cooked which should take 5-8 minutes
3. To serve, we recommend layering your burger patties in seeded burger buns with a generous dollop of sriracha or other chilli mayo, some lettuce, a slice of your favourite vegan cheese, and top with sliced tomato and red onion. Pair with chunky chips for a feel-good vegan treat!
4. Fun fact! Did you know that you can also cook frozen oven chips on your George Foreman! Simply put them onto your fully heated grill and cook with the lid down for 5-10 minutes before adding your burgers, and they should be ready at the same time! If you don't have space for both, cook the chips on their own for 8-15 minutes, depending on chunkiness. If you wanted a speedier cooking time, you can let the chips defrost on a baking tray first, then grill until crispy and fully cooked through.

DESSERTS RECIPES

Grilled Strawberry Maple Shortcake

Ingredients:

- 1 low fat shortcake, cut into 8 slices
- 60ml maple syrup
- 250g fresh strawberries, cleaned & sliced
- 250ml non fat whipped cream topping

Directions:

1. Preheat the grill, place the shortcake slices on the grill, brush with maple syrup and grill for 3 - 5 minutes, until the cake is toasted & completely warm.
2. Put the slices on individual plates, top with strawberries & cover with whipped topping.

Creme Egg Cookie Dough

Servings: 6-8 **Cooking Time: 20 Mins.**

Ingredients:

- 340g plain flour
- ¾ tsp bicarbonate of soda
- ½ tsp salt
- 225g butter, soft
- 120g light Muscovado sugar
- 120g golden caster sugar
- 3 tsp vanilla extract
- 2 large free range eggs
- 150g white chocolate chunks
- 150g milk chocolate chunks
- 6-8 crème eggs, roughly chopped

Directions:

1. Sift together the flour, bicarbonate of soda and salt in a bowl, set aside.
2. In a separate bowl, beat the butter, muscovado sugar and golden caster sugar together until light and fluffy.
3. Add the vanilla extract and eggs into the sugar mixture, and combine thoroughly.
4. Fold the sifted dry ingredients into the sugar mix, then add the chocolate chunks and Crème Eggs. Combine thoroughly, but don't overmix.
5. Lightly grease the deep pan plate of your George Foreman Evolve Grill, add the cookie dough and even out.
6. Attach the deep pan plate to the grill and cook on medium heat for 15-20 minutes.
7. Serve with your favourite ice cream while still hot, and dig in!

Air Fryer Ramekin Cookie

Servings: 1

Ingredients:

- ¼ cup flour
- 2 Tbsp. sugar
- ¼ tsp. baking powder
- ⅛ tsp. baking soda
- ⅛ tsp. salt
- 2 Tbsp. applesauce
- 2 Tbsp. milk
- 1 Tbsp. butter, melted
- ¼ tsp. vanilla
- 2 Tbsp. mini chocolate chips

Directions:

1. In a small bowl, whisk together the flour, sugar, baking powder and soda, and salt.
2. Make a hole in the center of the dry ingredients and add the applesauce, milk, butter and vanilla. Stir until combined. Fold in chocolate chips.
3. Pour batter into a greased ramekin and place in the air fryer bowl.
4. Tap the bake button and set temperature to 375°F and fry for 15 minutes until cookie is browned and cooked through.
5. Let cool and serve with a scoop of vanilla ice cream if desired.

Very Berry Cobbler

Servings: 8

Ingredients:

- 1 pkg. (16 oz.) frozen mixed berries
- 1 ½ cups (½ box) yellow cake mix
- 6 oz. lemon lime soda

Directions:

1. Securely attach the grill plate to the top of your grill and the baking pan to the bottom of your grill. Preheat grill to 325°F.
2. Spread the frozen fruit over bottom of baking pan.
3. Mix cake mix and seltzer water in medium bowl; pour over fruit.
4. Close grill top and bake 20 minutes or until cake is golden brown.

Notes:

1. Substitute white cake mix for yellow cake mix.
2. Substitute seltzer for lemon lime soda

Banana And Fudge Pancakes

Servings: 4-6 **Cooking Time:** 12 Mins.

Ingredients:

- 180g plain flour
- 3 tsp baking powder
- ½ tsp salt
- 30g golden caster sugar
- 2 large free range eggs
- 250ml milk
- 3 bananas
- 1 tsp vanilla extract
- 150g fudge pieces

Directions:

1. Sift the flour, baking powder, salt and sugar. Separately combine the milk, vanilla extract and egg yolks, puree 2 of the bananas and combine with the liquid. Mix the 2 together.
2. Dice the remaining banana into small chunks and stir into the mixture, along with the fudge pieces.
3. In a separate bowl, whisk the egg whites to stiff peak and fold into the mixture.
4. Pre heat the griddle side of your George Foreman Grill and Griddle, or alternatively a large greased frying pan. Spoon some of the mixture onto the griddle in even amounts and allow to cook for 1-3 minutes until the mixture starts to bubble. Flip over and cook for a further 1-3 minutes. Repeat until all of the mixture is cooked.
5. Serve with maple syrup.

Snickerdoodle Stuffed Croissant

Servings: 4

Ingredients:

- ½ tsp. ground cinnamon
- ½ cup cream cheese, softened
- 4 croissants
- 2 Tbsp. icing sugar

Directions:

1. Stir sugar with cinnamon until combined; set aside. Preheat your George Foreman Grill for 5 minutes with the lid closed. Meanwhile, slice croissants in half without cutting all the way through. Spread cream cheese evenly on bottom half of croissant and sprinkle 1 tsp cinnamon sugar over top. Cap with top half of croissant.
2. Place stuffed croissants on grill and cook for 2 to 3 minutes or until filling starts to ooze. Dust croissant with more cinnamon sugar.

Notes:

1. Serve with mixed berries, if desired.

George Foreman Grilled Peaches

Servings: 2

Ingredients:
- 1 Peach
- 1/8 tsp sugar

Directions:
1. Cut the peach in half and remove the pit
2. Sprinkle the peach with sugar
3. Grill the peach halves in the George Foreman Grill for ~5 minutes
4. Cut them up into salsas and desserts or puree them into sauces.

Grilled Stone Fruit | With Rice Pudding

Servings: 6

Ingredients:
- RICE PUDDING
- 2 cups water
- 2 cups unsweetened vanilla almond milk
- 1 (12 oz.) can evaporated milk
- ⅓ cup granulated sugar
- 1 tsp. cinnamon
- ¼ tsp. nutmeg
- ¼ tsp. salt
- 1 tsp. vanilla extract
- 1½ cup sushi rice
- GRILLED STONE FRUIT
- 2 medium peaches, cleaned, halved and pitted
- 2 nectarines, cleaned, halved and pitted
- 2 small plums, cleaned, halved and pitted
- 4 Tbsp. butter, melted
- 1 tsp. cinnamon
- 1 Tbsp. honey

Directions:
1. In a large saucepan, over medium-high heat, add water, almond milk, evaporated milk, sugar, cinnamon, nutmeg, salt and vanilla.
2. Bring to boil, stirring occasionally, until sugar is dissolved or about 15 minutes.
3. Turn heat down to low and add sushi rice. Stir and cover pan.
4. Cook rice until soft, about 15 minutes. Remove from heat, stir and place lid back on. Rice will continue to absorb liquid.
5. Meanwhile, preheat George Foreman grill by plugging it in, or setting it to MAX, 400°F or setting 4.
6. In a small bowl, combine melted butter, cinnamon and honey.
7. Brush inside half of each piece of fruit with butter mixture and place on preheated grill (butter side down).
8. Brush tops of fruit with remaining butter mixture and close lid.
9. Grill for 10 minutes. Flip fruit and continue to grill for ad ditional 5-6 minutes.
10. Stir rice pudding and pour into a large bowl or platter. Lay grilled stone fruit on top for family-style dessert.

Grilled Pears | With Honeyed Yogurt

 Servings: 4

Ingredients:

- 2 Tbsp. toasted chopped almonds
- 1 Tbsp. melted butter
- Pinch cinnamon
- 1 cup Greek yogurt
- 3 Tbsp. honey
- ½ tsp. finely grated lemon zest
- 4 ripe pears, halved and cored

Directions:

1. Preheat your George Foreman Grill for 5 minutes with the lid closed. Toss pear halves with melted butter. Place on grill, cut side down, and cook for 2 minutes. Turn and cook for an additional 1 to 2 minutes or until golden and tender
2. Meanwhile, stir yogurt with honey, lemon zest and cinnamon. Serve pears with honeyed yogurt and almonds. Drizzle with a little extra honey, if desired.
3. Tip: Serve with fresh raspberries for added fruit.

Peanut Butter Banana Panini

 Servings: 1

Ingredients:

- 1 small banana
- 1 slice bread ADD 1 slice bread + 100 calories
- 1 Tbsp. peanut butter ADD 1 Tbsp. peanut butter +

  100 calories
- ½ C. low-fat yogurt

Directions:

1. Preheat George Foreman® grill. Spread peanut butter on one half of the bread, top with sliced banana and fold. Place on George Foreman® grill for 4 minutes. Remove from grill, slice down the middle and enjoy.
2. For the Evolve Grill, preheat to 350° and cook for 4 minutes.
3. For the Indoor/Outdoor Grill, preheat to setting 3 and cook for 3-4 minutes per side.

Grilled Tiramisu Cake

 Servings: 4

Ingredients:

- 4 tsp. melted butter
- Chocolate shavings or cocoa powder
- 2 oz. strongly brewed espresso
- ½ cup mascarpone cheese
- 4 slices pound cake
- 2 Tbsp. granulated sugar
- 2 Tbsp. icing sugar
- 1 tsp. vanilla extract
- ½ cup whipped cream

Directions:

1. With electric beaters, beat mascarpone until light and fluffy. Beat in whipped cream, icing sugar and vanilla until smooth; keep chilled.
2. Preheat your George Foreman Grill for 5 minutes with the lid closed. Meanwhile, combine espresso with melted butter and sugar. Brush some onto both sides of pound cake slices. Place on grill and cook for approximately 2 minutes or until heated.
3. Brush slices with more espresso mixture. Place each pound cake slice on a dessert plate. Add dollop of whipped mascarpone topping. Garnish with chocolate shavings or cocoa powder.

Notes:
1. If you don't have espresso, use strong brewed coffee.

Vanilla Fruit Kebabs

Ingredients:

- 1 tin pineapple chunks
- 1 orange
- 1 banana
- 2 peaches / nectarines
- 1 tsp brown sugar
- 4 tbsp orange juice
- 1 tsp vanilla extract
- 8 x 10 inch wooden skewers
- 1 tsp vanilla extract
- For the quick creamy dip:
- 200ml fruit fromage frais
- 1 tsp vanilla extract

Directions:

1. Soak the skewers in water, then pat dry.
2. Cut the fruit into chunks and marinade for 10 minutes in the orange juice, brown sugar, and half the vanilla extract.
3. Thread the fruit chunks on the skewers. Grill for 4-6 minutes.
4. Mix the fromage frais with the remaining vanilla extract as a dip.

Pineapple Donut

Servings: 4

Ingredients:

- 4 tsp. melted butter
- 3 Tbsp. dulce de leche or caramel sauce, warmed
- Pinch cinnamon
- 4 plain 3-inch donuts, halved
- 4 pineapple rings, about ½ inch thick

Directions:

1. Preheat your George Foreman Grill for 5 minutes with the lid closed. Meanwhile, brush each pineapple ring with butter and sprinkle with cinnamon. Place on grill and cook for 2 to 3 minutes per side or until golden.
2. Sandwich a pineapple ring between donut halves to make a sandwich. Place each on a plate and drizzle with dulce de leche.

Notes:
1. Serve with blueberries and raspberries, if desired.

Whipped Goat Cheese Polenta Waffles

Servings: 7

Ingredients:

- 4 oz. herbed goat cheese
- 3½ cups milk, divided
- 1½ cups cornmeal
- &fac12; tsp. salt
- ¼ tsp. pepper
- 3 Tbsp. flour
- 3 Tbsp. cornstarch
- 1 egg

Directions:

1. Attach upper and lower waffle plates and preheat Grill & Broil to 425°F.
2. In medium bowl, whip goat cheese until smooth. Whisk in ½ cup milk until smooth and creamy.
3. In medium sauce pan, warm 3 cups milk over medium heat. Just before milk starts to bubble, slowly whisk in corn meal, ½ cup at time.
4. Continue to whisk until polenta starts to pull away from sides of pan, about 4-5 minutes.
5. Add polenta to goat cheese and stir to combine.
6. Add salt, pepper, flour, corn starch and egg. Stir to combine.
7. Spoon ½ cup of batter (batter will be thick) into center of each waffle plate and cook for 8 minutes.
8. Remove waffles and place on wire rack to cool. Repeat with remaining batter.

Notes:
1. Use as a base for meatballs and spaghetti sauce, or fried chicken with syrup.

Grilled Apple Cinnamon Skewers

 Servings: 4   Cooking Time: 10 Mins.

Ingredients:

- 4 tsp. melted butter
- 1 tsp. ground cinnamon
- 2 Granny Smith apples
- 2 red-skinned apples
- 3 Tbsp. granulated sugar

Directions:

1. Stir sugar with cinnamon until combined; set aside. Preheat your George Foreman Grill for 5 minutes with the lid closed. Meanwhile, cut each apple into 8 wedges. Thread evenly onto skewers. Brush skewers with butter then sprinkle with 1/2 tsp cinnamon sugar all over.
2. Place skewers on grill and cook for 2 minutes, turn and continue to cook for 1 to 2 minutes or until tender and golden. Sprinkle remaining cinnamon sugar onto each skewer. Serve warm.

Notes:
1. This recipe also works nicely with pears.

Grilled Pears | With Gingerbread Crumble

 Servings: 2

Ingredients:

- 1 Tbsp. brown sugar
- 1 Tbsp. butter, melted
- ¾ cup crumbled gingerbread cookies
- 6 small scoops vanilla ice cream
- 3 Bosc pears, peeled, halved and cored

Directions:

1. Preheat grill on sear setting. Toss pears with butter and brown sugar; grill for 5 minutes or until fork-tender.
2. Place each pear half on a plate. Top with vanilla ice cream and sprinkle with gingerbread cookie crumbs.

Notes:
1. Drizzle pears with caramel sauce before adding ice cream if desired.

Chocolate Brownies

Servings: 8-12 **Cooking Time:** 20 Mins.

Ingredients:

- Brownie
- 185g unsalted butter, melted
- 185g dark chocolate
- 275g golden caster sugar
- 3 large free range eggs
- 1 tsp vanilla extract
- 40g cocoa powder
- 85g plain flour
- 100g dark chocolate drops
- 100g white chocolate drops
- Topping
- 200g butter
- 150g white chocolate
- 280g icing sugar
- 1 tsp vanilla extract
- Popping candy

Directions:

1. Line the deep pan plate of your George Foreman Evolve Grill with baking paper, then attach to your grill and pre-heat to 1600
2. In a bowl, whisk together the eggs, sugar and vanilla extract until light and fluffy – this should take approximately 5-6 minutes.
3. In a small saucepan, heat the butter and chocolate together, stirring regularly until melted and fully combined. Leave to cool slightly for a few minutes.
4. Gradually pour the chocolate into the sugary egg mixture, whisking continuously. Once combined, sieve in the flour and cocoa powder, then slowly fold into the wet mixture making sure it is well combined but do not overmix. Finally, fold in the chocolate drops.
5. Pour the mix into your deep pan plate and spread it out to an even thickness all over. Cook for approximately 25 minutes, then turn off and leave too cool in the deep pan.
6. In a bowl, whisk together add the butter and vanilla until it starts to turn white and fluffy. Melt the chocolate in the microwave and into the butter, whisking continuously. Add the sugar and mix well.
7. Once the brownie has cooled cut into equal portions and using a piping bag pipe a little of the topping onto each portion. Sprinkle with the popping candy.

Lemon Poppy Seed Cake | With Plum Topping

Servings: 10

Ingredients:

- 1 box (15.6 oz.) Quick Bread and Muffin Mix
- 1 ripe red plum, cut into ½-inch pieces

Directions:

1. Insert baking pan in contact roaster. Preheat 5 minutes.
2. Prepare quick bread mix according to package directions. Lightly grease bottom and sides of baking pan. Pour batter into baking pan top with plum slices.
3. Set timer and bake, covered 30 minutes. Turn off roaster and allow cake to rest in roaster 10 minutes.

Notes:

1. Drizzle a thin icing of powdered sugar and milk over the cake before serving.

Cookie Dough

Servings: 6-8 **Cooking Time: 20 Mins.**

Ingredients:

- 225g butter, soft
- 120g light Muscovado sugar
- 120g golden caster sugar
- 3 tsp vanilla extract
- 2 large free range eggs
- 340g plain flour
- ¾ tsp bicarbonate of soda
- ½ tsp salt
- 150g white chocolate chunks
- 150g milk chocolate chunks

Directions:

1. Sift the flour, bicarbonate of soda and salt into a bowl.
2. In a separate large bowl, beat together the butter, Muscovado sugar and golden caster sugar until light and fluffy. Add each egg one at a time, beating thoroughly in between. Then mix in the vanilla extract.
3. Carefully fold the dry ingredients into the butter mix and stir through the chocolate chunks.
4. Lightly grease the deep pan plate and tip in the cookie dough. Spread evenly and make sure the dough reaches the sides.
5. Attach the deep pan plate to the grill and cook on medium heat for 15-20 minutes, checking periodically to ensure it doesn't burn.
6. Serve hot with a scoop of vanilla ice cream.

Grilled American Doughnuts

Servings: 2-4 **Cooking Time: 10 Mins.**

Ingredients:

- 2-4 ring doughnuts
- Whipped cream
- Strawberries
- Optional:
- Chocolate, melted

Directions:

1. Pre-heat your favourite George Foreman Grill to maximum.
2. Place each whole doughnut on the grill, close the lid and cook for 1-2 minutes, or until the outside begins to char and crisp up.
3. Remove your grilled doughnuts and serve with your favourite dessert toppings – we recommend whipped cream and fresh strawberries, but your favourite ice cream and a drizzle of melted chocolate would be delicious too!

PORK RECIPES

Hot Sausage Sandwiches

👥 Servings: 5

Ingredients:

- 1 large garlic clove, finely minced
- 1 tsp. dried Italian seasoning
- ¼ tsp. black pepper, coarsely ground
- 1 lb. low-fat hot Italian sausage links
- 1 tomato, sliced
- 1 green pepper, seeded & thinly sliced
- 1 small purple onion, thinly sliced
- ¼ cup non-fat mayonnaise
- 4 sandwich buns, split & toasted

Directions:

1. In a small bowl, combine the garlic, Italian seasoning and pepper; sprinkle the mixture over sausages and vegetables.
2. Arrange the sausages horizontally on a preheated grill and place the tomato, green pepper and onion around the links. Grill for 6 minutes, or until a meat thermometer inserted into center of the sausage registers 160° F.
3. Spread mayonnaise on the bottom of each bun and add the sausage and vegetable mixture. Top with remaining half of bun.
4. USING OTHER GRILLS
5. For the Evolve grill preheat to 350° and place all ingredients on the grill for 4-6 minutes.
6. For the Indoor/Outdoor Grill, set grill to preheat at Setting 4 and place ingredients on the grill and cook for 5-7 minutes while covered.

Bacon Wrapped Stuffed Jalapeno Peppers & Yoghurt Dip

👥 Servings: 12   🕐 Cooking Time: 10 Mins.

Ingredients:

- 10-12 jalapeno peppers
- 10-12 smoked streaky bacon slices
- 150-200g cream cheese
- 80g cheddar cheese, finely grated
- 1 shallot, finely diced
- ½ tsp smoked paprika
- Salt and pepper to taste

Directions:

1. Combine the cream cheese and grated cheeses, shallot, paprika and seasoning together.
2. Cut the peppers in half lengthways and scoop out the seeds.
3. Divide the cheese mixture evenly and fill one-half of each of the peppers. Place the other half of each pepper back on top of the filled half of the pepper.
4. Lay out a piece of bacon, then lay a stuffed pepper on one end of the bacon slice and wrap the pepper in the piece of bacon. Repeat this for all the peppers.
5. Pre heat you Small Fit Grill. Cook the peppers in two batches for 6-8 minutes.
6. Serve with a yoghurt - dip we like to use tzatziki.

Sweet Bbq Veggie Pulled 'pork' Quesadilla (vegetarian)

Servings: 1

Ingredients:

- 1 wholemeal wrap,
- 1 Linda McCartney BBQ pulled 'pork' 1/4 pounder, pre-cooked
- Half a crushed baked or microwaved sweet potato (around 80g),
- 25 g 50% reduced fat cheddar cheese,
- 1 small green chilli, sliced and seeds left in,
- 1 tbsp BBQ sauce (I used HP),
- Salt and pepper to season
- Olive oil Frylight
- You will need:
- 1 George Foreman grill or griddle/frying pan

Directions:

1. Take the wrap and lay it out. Using the back of a table spoon take the baked sweet potato flesh from the skin and spread it out evenly over half of the wrap. Season with salt and pepper.
2. Next sprinkle over half the grated cheese and the chillies.
3. Take the quarter pounder and shred it into small pieces on a chopping board then sprinkle it evenly over the half of the wrap with the sweet potato.
4. Drizzle over the BBQ sauce and then sprinkle over the remaining cheese.
5. Fold over the other half of the wrap so it neatly covers the half where you've added the ingredients.
6. Now spray both sides with Frylight and place onto the grill (or frying pan). If cooking on a George Foreman, allow to heat for around 5 minutes until the inside is piping hot. If using a pan, cook on one side for around 2-3 minutes then flip it and cook the other side.
7. Allow to cool for about 2 minutes then eat and enjoy! :)
8. Each quesadilla is approximately 477kcals.

Brussels Sprouts With Chestnuts And Bacon

Cooking Time: 20 Mins.

Ingredients:

- 750g sprouts, trimmed
- 1½ tbsp olive oil
- 8-10 rashers smoked streaky bacon
- 200g vacuum packed chestnuts, chopped
- Salt and pepper to taste

Directions:

1. In a pan, cook the sprouts in boiling salted water for 2-3 minutes. Drain and plunge into iced water to cool.
2. Once fully cooled, drain again then dry thoroughly on kitchen paper.
3. Pre-heat your favourite George Foreman Grill to maximum, and once up to temperature, cook the bacon for 5-8 minutes until crispy. Set aside to cool slightly, then chop into small pieces.
4. Cut the sprouts in half and toss them in the olive oil and season then grill until charred and cooked through.
5. Combine the grilled halved sprouts, bacon and chopped chestnuts.

Apricot, Cranberry, Sage And Sausage Stuffing Balls

⏱ Cooking Time: 15 Mins.

Ingredients:

- 800-900g pork sausage meat
- 140g dried apricots, chopped
- 100g dried cranberries, chopped
- 4 shallots, finely chopped
- 3 cloves garlic, finely chopped
- ½ bunch sage, chopped
- 100g breadcrumbs
- Salt and pepper to taste

Directions:

1. In a large bowl, mix all ingredients together, ensuring it is all thoroughly combined and there are no hidden pockets of dry ingredients.
2. Divide the mixture into equal amounts and roll into balls approximately the size of a golf ball.
3. Pre-heat your favourite George Foreman Grill to maximum. Once up to temperature, place 6 – 8 stuffing balls on to your grill (or as many that will comfortably fit) and cook for 10-15 minutes until they are fully cooked through, turning every so often so they are browned all over.
4. Repeat until all the stuffing balls are cooked.

Honey Bbq Pork | & Pineapple Skewers

👥 Servings: 10   ⏱ Cooking Time: 8 Mins.

Ingredients:

- 1 ½ lb. pork tenderloin, cut into 1" cubes
- Salt & Pepper
- 4 cups chopped pineapple
- ½ cup honey BBQ sauce
- 10 (10") bamboo skewers

Directions:

1. Preheat the Indoor/Outdoor grill on Setting 4.
2. Season pork with salt and pepper. Place one cube of pork on a skewer, followed by one piece of pineapple, alternating until the skewer is full. Repeat with the remaining skewers.
3. Brush one side of each skewer with BBQ sauce and lay BBQ sauce side down on the preheated grill. Brush the top side with BBQ sauce and place the lid on the grill.
4. Grill the skewers for 4 minutes per side. Serve immediately.

Cuban Pita

👪 Servings: 6

Ingredients:

- 3 precut & ready to fill pita pockets
- Yellow mustard
- 6 oz. deli sliced ham
- 6 sandwich pickles
- 9 oz. sliced pork
- 3 slices Swiss cheese, cut in half

Directions:

1. Preheat the Indoor/Outdoor Grill on Setting 4.
2. Cut each pita in half. Carefully open the pita, making sure not to break either side.
3. Spread a thin layer of yellow mustard on one side of the pita. Place one half of Swiss cheese on top of the mustard. Place a pickle on top of the cheese.
4. Fill with 1 oz sliced ham and 1 ½ oz. pork. Repeat with the remaining pitas.
5. Place the pitas on the preheated grill. Place the lid on the grill.
6. Grill the pitas for 6 minutes per side, until cheese is melted.
7. Serve warm with black beans and rice or tortilla chips.

Honey Mustard Pork Chops

👪 Servings: 2

Ingredients:

- 1 lb. pork loin chops
- 1 Tbsp. honey mustard
- ½ Tbsp. honey
- ⅛ tsp. garlic powder
- ⅛ tsp. onion powder
- Salt & Pepper to taste

Directions:

1. Preheat the Indoor/Outdoor grill on Setting 4. In a small bowl mix together the honey mustard, honey, garlic powder, onion powder and salt and pepper.
2. Pat pork loins dry with a paper towel and season with your favorite pork rub (I love a sweet and smoky rub to bring out the sweetness of the honey).
3. Place pork chops onto the preheated grill and place the lid on the grill. Grill for 5-7 minutes. Flip pork chops and baste the grilled side with the honey mustard mix. Place the lid back on the grill and continue grilling for 3-4 minutes. Flip the pork chops and baste the remaining side. Place the lid back on the grill and continue to cook for 1-2 more minutes.
4. Once the pork chops have reached an internal temperature of 135°F, take off the grill and let rest for 5 minutes, until the internal temperature reaches 145°F.

Greek Pork Chops

Servings: 4

Ingredients:

- ¼ tsp. dried basil
- 4 pork ribeye chops, ¼" thick
- ¼ cup olive oil
- ¼ tsp. onion powder
- ¼ tsp. dried oregano
- ½ tsp. dried thyme
- ¼ tsp. garlic powder
- ½ tsp. salt
- ¼ tsp. pepper
- ½ cup feta cheese crumbles
- 3 cups cooked orzo
- ½ cup Kalamata olives, sliced
- 1 cup artichoke hearts, quartered
- ½ cup roasted red peppers, chopped
- 1 cup English cucumber, chopped
- ¼ cup Italian dressing

Directions:

1. In zip-top bag, combine oil, oregano, basil, thyme, onion, garlic powder, salt and pepper. Seal bag and shake to combine.
2. Place pork chops in bag, seal and massage in marinade.
3. Marinate pork chops in refrigerator for 30 minutes prior to cooking.
4. Meanwhile, in large bowl, mix together cooked orzo, olives, artichoke hearts, roasted red peppers, cucumber and dressing. Toss to combine. Cover and place in refrigerator.
5. Attach upper and lower grill plates. Preheat Grill & Broil to 400°F.
6. Remove pork chops and place on preheated grill. Grill for 4 minutes or until internal temperature of 145°F is reached.
7. Carefully remove upper grill plate and top each pork chop with crumbled feta. Cook on HIGH Broil for 2 to 3 minutes, or until cheese is softencd.
8. Remove pork chops and allow to rest for 5 to 10 minutes before slicing.

Notes:
1. Spoon pasta salad on to four plates and top each with pork chop.

Grilled Pork Cutlet With Rosemary

Servings: 4

Ingredients:

- 1 1/2 pound boneless pork cutlet
- 2 lemons, juiced
- 2 tablespoons olive oil
- 2 tablespoons honey
- 1/2 teaspoon dried rosemary
- salt and pepper, to taste

Directions:

1. Place the cutlet between two sheets of wax paper and pound thin with a meat hammer or the bottom of a heavy skillet.
2. Combine the lemon juice, olive oil, honey, rosemary and pepper in a small shallow bowl and mix well. Add the pork cutlet and refrigerate for 1 hour, turning the meat occasionally.
3. Preheat the grill and brush with oil. Remove the meat from the marinade and grill, basting occasionally, for 4-6 minutes.

Bbq Pork Ribs

⏱ Cooking Time: 20 Mins.

Ingredients:

- 1 rack baby back ribs, boiled in water with 2 tbsp salt until tender, making sure to keep the rack whole (approx. 2-3 hours)
- For the BBQ sauce –
- ½ white onion, finely chopped
- 1 clove garlic, finely chopped
- 60g tomato ketchup
- 10ml dark soy sauce
- 1 tbsp dark brown sugar
- 1 tbsp Worcestershire sauce
- ½ tbsp malt vinegar
- 3-4 drops tabasco sauce
- ¼ tsp mustard powder
- 2 tbsp olive oil

Directions:

1. For the BBQ sauce, attach the deep pan plate to your George Foreman Evolve Grill and pre-heat to 2200 Add the oil and heat for 1 minute.
2. Add the diced onion and garlic to your grill and cook for 3-4 minutes until they become translucent, stirring occasionally.
3. Carefully add the ketchup, soy sauce, sugar, Worcestershire sauce, vinegar, tabasco and mustard powder, and stir well. Cook for 4-5 minutes, stirring occasionally. Then, turn the grill off and allow the sauce to cool. Transfer to a bowl and set aside for later.
4. Clean the deep pan plate and refit it to the grill. Pre-heat to 1750 Place the ribs into the deep pan plate and spoon ½ - ¾ of the BBQ sauce over the top and reserve the rest – make sure the ribs are fully coated by spreading the BBQ sauce over with a brush or the back of a spoon.
5. Add 100ml of hot water and cook for 20-30 minutes with the lid closed. Check occasionally to make sure the water hasn't dried up. If it has, add some more water.
6. Remove from the grill and serve up with the remaining BBQ sauce drizzled over the top. Pair with buttery grilled corn on the cob, a leafy green salad and a potato salad for a delicious feast worth getting your hands dirty for.

Apricot-glazed Pork Chops

Servings: 3

Ingredients:

- ⅓ cup apricot preserves
- 2 pork chops
- ¼ cup white wine
- 1 sprig fresh rosemary
- Salt and pepper to taste

Directions:

1. Mix apricot preserves and white wine in small bowl.
2. Remove top grill plate from George Foreman® Grill & Broil and turn to "Broil" mode.
3. Place two pork chops on lower plate and sprinkle with salt and pepper. Allow to broil for 3-4 minutes.
4. Turn pork chops over. Spoon apricot mixture over top of pork chops then allow to broil for 3-4 more minutes.
5. Remove from broiler and allow to sit for 2 minutes. Garnish with any remaining sauce and serve!

FISH AND SEAFOOD RECIPES

George Foreman Grilled Catfish

Servings: 4

Ingredients:

- 2 pounds catfish filets
- seasoned salt to taste
- lemon pepper
- olive oil

Directions:

1. Heat grill for about 2 minutes. In a large bowl, place fillets and season with salt, and lemon pepper. Coat generously with olive oil. Sprinkle a bit more lemon pepper. Place on grill and let cook for about ten minutes.
2. Cook's Notes: I usually grill about four fillets at a time on a family sized grill. I also tend to like my fillets cooked a little longer. This recipe has been a huge success for me at dinners and get-togethers.

Lemon And Parsley Stuffed Grilled Trout

Servings: 4

Ingredients:

- 4 butterflied trout
- 5 lemon slices per fish
- 6-8 fresh parsley leaves per fish
- 2 garlic cloves per fish
- Salt and pepper
- Can be made using any George Foreman grill – we recommend the Large Fit Grill or Smokeless BBQ Grill.

Directions:

1. Open up the trout and check there are no bones left inside by lightly running your finger over the flesh, then season both sides with salt and pepper. Lay lemon slices and pieces of parsley within the open fish, alternating between them. Peel and roughly chop the garlic and sprinkle over the top of them lemon and parsley, and drizzle with olive oil. Close the fish.
2. Heat your favourite George Foreman Grill to maximum and cook the lemon and parsley stuffed trout for 5-8 minutes, depending on thickness of the fish.
3. Serve with your favourite seasonal sides – we recommend boiled new potatoes and Tenderstem broccoli!
4. Top tip – in most supermarkets with a fish monger they should be able to butterfly the trout for you!

Grilled Chilli Prawns With Lettuce And Polenta

Servings: 4 **Cooking Time:** 20 Mins.

Ingredients:

- 4-6 large raw prawns per person (tails on)
- Sweet chilli sauce
- Olive oil
- 4 little gem lettuces
- Handful of pitted black olives (of your choice, dried are best)
- 1 packet pre-cooked polenta
- 12 mini plum tomatoes

Directions:

1. Pre-heat your George Foreman Grill until ready.
2. Slice the polenta into 8 slices and brush lightly with olive oil and place on the grill for 5 mins.
3. Place the prawns in a bowl with 1 desert spoonful each of sweet chilli sauce and olive oil. Turn in the mix carefully and leave to marinate.
4. Cut the little gems in two lengthwise, brush with a little of the prawn marinade and place on the grill.
5. Turn the polenta to cook on the reverse side. Thread the prawns onto short wooden skewers and place on the grill.
6. Cut the tomatoes in half and place in a bowl with the olives.
7. Remove the grilled lettuce when golden brown on the cut side.
8. Once the prawns are sticky and golden remove from the skewers and add to the salad .
9. Place the grilled polenta on a plate and top with the salad. Make a quick dressing from the chilli sauce and olive oil to taste and drizzle over. Add salt and pepper as needed.

Notes:
1. Serve without the polenta for a delicious starter

Cajun Shrimp

Servings: 6

Ingredients:

- 41-50 shrimp, peeled
- ½ tsp salt
- 1 tsp. pepper
- 1 Tbsp. garlic powder
- 1 tsp. onion powder
- 1 Tbsp paprika
- 1 tsp. cayenne
- 1 tsp. thyme
- 1 tsp. oregano
- ½ tsp. red pepper flakes

Directions:

1. Preheat the Indoor/Outdoor grill on setting 5.
2. In a small bowl, combine all ingredients, except the shrimp.
3. Place the shrimp in a zip top bag and sprinkle in 1 tablespoon of the Cajun seasoning mix. Reserve the rest of the seasoning for another time.
4. Skewer 5 pieces of shrimp onto one skewer, repeating until the shrimp is gone.
5. Place the shrimp skewers onto the preheated grill. Place the lid on the grill. Grill for2 minutes per side.
6. Serve on top of rice or pasta.

Honey Cumin Fish Tacos

Servings: 8

Ingredients:

- TACOS & MARINADE
- ¼ cup soy sauce
- 2 Tbsp. honey
- ½ tsp. ground ginger
- 1 tsp. cumin
- 1 Tbsp. fresh squeezed lime juice
- 8 tilapia fillets
- Salt and pepper
- 8 flour tortillas
- Lime slices and cilantro for garnish as desired
- CILANTRO LIME COLESLAW
- 2 Tbsp. chopped cilantro
- 1 (14 oz.) bag coleslaw
- 1 cup Greek yogurt
- 1 Tbsp. honey
- 2 Tbsp. fresh squeezed lime juice
- Salt and pepper to taste

Directions:

1. In a shallow dish or bowl, mix together the soy sauce, honey, ginger, cumin, and lime juice.
2. Season the tilapia fillets with salt and pepper and lay them in the marinade, turning to coat each side. Cover and place in the refrigerator for at least 30 minutes.
3. Meanwhile, in a large bowl, mix together coleslaw ingredients. Cover and refrigerate until ready to serve.
4. If using the Indoor/Outdoor Grill, preheat it using setting 3.
5. Place the marinated fillets on the preheated grill and lower the lid.
6. Grill for 2 minutes per side.
7. Place one fillet in each tortilla, top with the cilantro lime coleslaw, add garnish and serve

Prawn Skewers

Servings: 2-4   Cooking Time: 20 Mins.

Ingredients:

- 4-8 skewers
- 8 large king prawns, peeled
- 2 red onions, roughly diced
- 2 red peppers, cut into rough dice
- 8 cherry tomatoes
- 3 tbsp olive oil
- Salt and pepper to taste

Directions:

1. Firstly, soak your wooden skewers in water for 30 minutes so they don't burn once on the grill.
2. On each wooden skewer, thread on the prawns, cherry tomatoes, red pepper and red onion, alternating throughout. Repeat until all skewers are filled and set aside.
3. Pre-heat your favourite George Foreman Grill.
4. Brush the skewers with the olive oil and season to taste.
5. Cook each skewer for 8-12 minutes until cooked through.
6. Serve with your favourite dips - we recommend sweet chilli or Sriracha.

Grilled Shrimp With Southwestern Black Bean Salad

 Servings: 6   Cooking Time: 10 Mins.

Ingredients:

- ***Marinated Shrimp***
- 1/3 cup fresh lime juice
- 1/4 cup thawed orange juice concentrate
- 2 tablespoons low-sodium soy sauce
- 2 tablespoons Worcestershire sauce
- 2 tablespoons honey
- 1 clove garlic, minced
- 2 pounds large shrimp, peeled
- non-stick cooking spray
- ***Salad***
- 2 cups coarsely chopped tomato
- 1/2 cup sliced green onions
- 1/3 cup chopped fresh cilantro
- 1 can (15 ounce size) black beans, rinsed and drained
- 1 can (15.25 ounce size) whole-kernel corn, drained
- 1 jalapeno pepper, seeded and chopped
- 1/4 cup fresh lime juice
- 2 tablespoons olive oil
- 1/2 teaspoon cumin
- 1/4 teaspoon salt
- 1/8 teaspoon black pepper

Directions:

1. To prepare marinated shrimp, combine first 6 ingredients in a large zip-top bag. Add shrimp to bag; seal. Marinate in refrigerator 1 hour, turning occasionally. Remove shrimp from bag; discard marinade.
2. Preheat George Foreman grill.
3. Place shrimp on grill coated with cooking spray. Grill 1-2 minutes or until shrimp are done (check after one minute).
4. To prepare salad, combine tomato and next 5 ingredients (tomato through jalapeno) in a large bowl. Combine 1/4 cup lime juice, oil, cumin, salt, and black pepper in a small bowl; stir with a whisk. Pour dressing over bean mixture; toss well. Spoon salad onto each of 6 plates; top with shrimp.

Classic Crab Cakes

 Servings: 8

Ingredients:

- ¾ cup bread crumbs
- ¼ cup mayonnaise
- 1 Tbsp. olive oil
- 2 Tbsp. finely chopped parsley
- 2 green onions, finely chopped
- 2 Tbsp. Dijon mustard
- 1 Tbsp. lemon juice
- 1 tsp. Worcestershire sauce
- ½ lb. flaked crabmeat (fresh or canned)
- TARTAR SAUCE
- 2 tsp. fresh lemon juice
- ½ cup light mayonnaise
- 2 tsp. Dijon mustard
- 4 cornichon pickles, minced
- Pinch each salt and freshly ground black pepper
- 1 small shallot, minced

Directions:

1. Tartar Sauce: Stir together mayonnaise, pickles, mustard, lemon juice, shallot, salt and pepper. Cover and refrigerate for at least 30 minutes until chilled or for up to 1 week.
2. Place griddle plates on the grill. Use switch at bottom right rear of grill to make flat surface. Close cover; set cooking temperature at 400°F and cooking time for 10 minutes. Allow grill to preheat for 5 minutes.
3. Stir together 1/2 cup of the bread crumbs, mayonnaise, parsley, green onions, mustard, lemon juice and Worcestershire sauce. Crumble in crabmeat; stir to combine. Shape into 8 balls and press into 1/2-inch patties.
4. Place remaining bread crumbs in a shallow dish. Carefully press each patty into crumbs to coat. Brush lightly with oil; grill, turning once, for 10 minutes or until golden brown on the outside and heated though. Serve with tartar sauce.

Notes:

1. Extra tartar sauce can be served with grilled fish fillets or mixed with canned tuna for a quick sandwich filling.
2. For the Indoor/Outdoor Grill: preheat grill to setting 3 and cook covered for 3 minutes per side.
3. For Classic Plate Grill: preheat the grill, and cook crab cakes for 4-5 minutes.

Lowfat Salmon Patties George Foreman Grill

 Servings: 4

Ingredients:

- 1 large can pink salmon
- 2 Egg Beaters (or eggs if you prefer)
- 1 chopped onion
- 1/2 cup low fat cracker crumbs
- OR
- 1/4 cup flour
- 1 teaspoon salt (optional)
- freshly ground black pepper (optional)

Directions:

1. Flake salmon with a fork. Whip egg beaters and add to salmon. Sir in crumbs or flour and onion and salt and mix well.
2. Form into patties. Spray each side of patty with nonstick cooking spray and place in George Foreman grill. Brown on each side.

Grilled Salmon On The George Foreman Grill

Servings: 4

Ingredients:

- 1/4 cup freshly squeezed lemon juice
- 2 tablespoons olive oil, more for the grill
- 2 tablespoons finely chopped fresh oregano
- 2 tablespoons coarsely chopped fresh thyme
- 2 tablespoons finely chopped fresh basil
- 1 teaspoon sea salt
- 1/2 teaspoon freshly ground black pepper
- 2 pounds salmon fillets

Directions:

1. Gather the ingredients.
2. In a non-reactive bowl, whisk together lemon juice, 1 tablespoon olive oil, herbs, salt, and pepper.
3. Rinse the salmon under cold water, and then pat it dry with a paper towel or clean kitchen towel.
4. Add salmon to the olive mixture, turning to coat well. Let the salmon marinate while you preheat the George Foreman (or any indoor contact) grill.
5. Place the salmon on George Foreman grill. Cook for 3 to 8 minutes. The cooking time will depend on the thickness of the salmon.

Notes:

1. The George Foreman tends to cook much faster than a regular grill, so check salmon at 3 minutes. If the salmon easily flakes when poked with a fork and is opaque throughout, it's done.
2. If you don't have an indoor electric grill, you can also cook this salmon on a grill pan on the stove.
3. All cuts of fresh salmon will have pin bones, which are the fish's rib bones. It's easy to choke on these bones, so they should be removed. Lay the fish skin-side-down and run your fingers over the fillet; in most cases, you should feel the bones sticking out of the fish. Pull them straight up with clean tweezers or small kitchen pliers.
4. If you're getting a little bit of white stuff on the flesh of your salmon as it cooks, don't worry too much. It's albumin, a protein that shows up from the fish's muscle fibers as it cooks, and it occurs on even perfectly cooked fish. However, it shows up more often on overcooked fish, so only keep the salmon on the grill for a minimum amount of time to minimize albumin formation.

Fish Finger Sandwich

Servings: 1 **Cooking Time:** 10 Mins.

Ingredients:

- 3 slice of thick white bread
- 6 frozen fish fingers
- 4-5 leaves of little gem lettuce
- 2 tbsp. tartar sauce

Directions:

1. Pre-heat your favourite George foreman Grill.
2. While your grill is heating, prep your slices of bread by lathering on a thick layer of tartar sauce on two or all of the slices, then lay a few leaves of lettuce on two of the slices.
3. Lay your frozen fish fingers on the grill for around 8-10 minutes or until they are cooked through and piping hot.
4. Construct your sandwich. Layer one slice of bread with lettuce, 3 fish fingers, and 1tbsp tartar sauce. Repeat and top with the remaining slice of bread.

Szechwan Tuna Steaks

Servings: 4

Ingredients:

- 4 tuna steaks, approx 1 inch thick
- 60ml soy sauce
- 2tbsp rice vinegar
- 1tsp sugar
- 1tbsp dark sesame oil
- 1tbsp hot chili oil
- 1 clove garlic, crushed
- 3tbsp coriander, chopped

Directions:

1. Place tuna in single layer in a large shallow glass dish.
2. In a small bowl, combine the soy sauce, vinegar, sugar, sesame oil, hot chili oil and garlic, mixing well.
3. Set aside 2tbsp of mixture and pour remaining over the tuna steaks. Cover with cling film and refrigerate 40 minutes, turning over once.
4. Preheat the grill to maximum temperature and grill for 4-6 minutes until tuna is opaque but still feels somewhat soft in centre.
5. Cut each tuna steak into thin slices (lengthwise) and fan out onto plates.
6. Drizzle tuna slices with reserved sauce and sprinkle with coriander.
7. Tip: Serve with a fresh salad for a light lunch or with noodles and stir fried veg for a main meal.
8. If you are using a George Foreman Evolve grill, use the 'sear' function to achieve a perfectly cooked tuna steak.

Grilled Tuna Salad Nicoise

Servings: 2   **Cooking Time:** 15 Mins.

Ingredients:

- 2 tuna steaks
- Olive oil
- 2 boiled eggs, cut in quarters
- 6-8 green beans, cooked in salted water
- 10-12 cherry tomatoes, cut in half
- Kalamata olives, sliced
- Lettuce leaves
- Salt and pepper to taste

Directions:

1. Bring a pan of water to the boil, and cook your eggs to the desired runniness – around 4 minutes for runny and 6-8 minutes for set yolks. Once cooked, run under the cold tap to stop the cooking process and set aside for later.
2. Pre-heat your favourite George Foreman Grill to maximum. Brush tuna steaks with olive oil and season with salt and pepper, and place each on the grill.
3. Cook the tuna steaks with the lid down for 4-8 minutes, or to your liking – don't forget, your tuna steaks will cook faster in the grill than you might be used to in a pan, so make sure to keep an eye on them!
4. To assemble the salad, place a bed of lettuce into your bowls and top with the green beans, cherry tomatoes and olives. Then halve or quarter your boiled eggs and gently place on top, then add the cooked tuna steaks and you're ready to dig in!

Curried Fish Goujons

Servings: 2-4   **Cooking Time:** 10 Mins.

Ingredients:

- For the fish goujons:
- large tuna, cod or salmon steak cut into strips
- 25g wholemeal flour
- 1 egg white
- 1 slice of fresh wholemeal bread broken into breadcrumbs
- 1 tsp white pepper
- ½ tsp medium curry powder (leave out if preferred)

Directions:

1. Cut the fish into evenly sized strips.
2. In a bowl, mix together the flour, curry powder & pepper. Put the egg white in a separate bowl, and the breadcrumbs in a third bowl.
3. Firstly, dip the fish strips into the seasoned flour, then into the egg white & then into the breadcrumbs until well coated.
4. Pre-hear your favourite George Foreman Grill and cook for 3-5 minutes, depending on the thickness of your fish.
5. Serve with a squeeze of lemon and some tartar sauce for a delicious dinner party appetizer that'll get everyone talking!

OTHER FAVORITE RECIPES

George Foreman Evolve Grill Pizza

Ingredients:

- 1 can refrigerated pizza dough
- 10 oz cheese
- 1 can Marinara or Pizza Sauce
- Toppings of choice
- 1 tbsp EVOO
- to taste seasonings

Directions:

1. In the Evolve Grill change the bottom griddle plate to the baking pan. For ease in removing and clean-up take parchment paper and line the pan, with some over lapping, for ease in transfer to a cutting board. Leave the top griddle plate in place. You don't have to pre-heat the unit.
2. Open pizza dough and fit into the baking pan. Brush a little of the EVOO over the dough. Spread with appox. 1 cp of the marinara or pizza sauce (I have made this twice. The second time I used much less sauce). Start loading on your toppings. If using any meat, such as ground beef, pork, sausage or chicken, make sure to pre-cook.
3. Season to taste.
4. Add cheese. Used sliced the first time and shredded the second. They both worked.
5. Take the excess parchment paper (rear of grill) and pull over entire pizza. Close lid and cook at 400°F. for about 20 - 25 mins.
6. When browned and cheese has melted (YES, you will probably have grill marks) use parchment paper to help remove and place on cutting board.

Bacon-wrapped Apps

Servings: 20

Ingredients:

- 10 Slices of Bacon, cut in half
- 10 Pieces of one (or combination) of the following
- 10 Pinapple Chunks
- 10 Scallops
- 10 Large Cooked Shrimp, peeled and deveined
- 10 Whole Water Chestnuts

Directions:

1. Wrap bacon around your choice of shrimp, scallops, water chestnuts or pineapple. Secure with toothpicks.
2. Preheat the George Foreman® Contact Roaster.
3. Using tongs, carefully place wrapped appetizers directly in the roaster. Set timer and cook 10 minutes.
4. Turn appetizers over and cook an additional 5 to 10 minutes, or until heated through and bacon is browned. Serve immediately.

Croque Monsieur

Cooking Time: 10 Mins.

Ingredients:

- 4 slices bread
- 8 slices ham
- 8 slices Swiss cheese
- Sunflower oil spray

Directions:

1. Pre heat the grill to maximum.
2. Take 2 slices of the bread and spray both sides with the sunflower oil spray. Layer 4 slices of ham and 4 slices of cheese on each slice. Take the remaining 2 slices of bread and spray with sunflower oil spray. Place on top of the ham and cheese.
3. Place on the grill and cook for 5- 10 minutes until the bread is golden brown.

Five Spice Duck

Servings: 4

Ingredients:

- 4 x 200g duck breasts – approximate
- 4 tsp. 5 spice
- 30g dark brown sugar
- 6 garlic cloves
- 60ml dark soy sauce

Directions:

1. Trim away any excess fat and skin off the top of the duck breast leaving just enough to cover the meat with no additional around the sides, then carefully score the skin with a sharp knife - this is much easier if the duck is chilled.
2. Finely chop the garlic and put in a bowl, then add the five spice, sugar and soy sauce, and mix. Add the duck breasts and mix well, then cover with cling film and leave to marinate for at least 2 hours or overnight if you have the time.
3. Heat your favourite George Foreman grill to maximum and cook the duck for 7-8 minutes, depending on the size

Notes:

1. take the duck out of the fridge at least 30-40 minutes before cooking to come up to room temperature, as this will result in more tender meat.

George Foreman Reheat Frozen Burritos

Servings: 2

Ingredients:
- Frozen Burritos
- Foil

Directions:
1. The burrito will get a bit flattened by the grill, so rewrap it in foil if you think it may explode.
2. Grill the burrito for 10 minutes if thawed, 20 minutes if frozen. Depends on the size of the burrito too.

Grilled Ham & Cheese Bagel

Servings: 2

Ingredients:
- 2 bagels
- 4 slices American cheese
- 2 ounces shaved ham

Directions:
1. Preheat George Foreman grill for 5 minutes.
2. Place bagel tops on the grill. Close the lid and heat for 3 minutes. Remove bagel tops from the grill and keep warm.
3. Place 2 slices of cheese on each bagel bottom. Top with the ham.
4. Place on the grill and close the cover. Allow to cook for 3 minutes.
5. Remove from the grill and top with the bagel top.

Hoisin Duck Pancakes

Servings: 3-4   **Cooking Time:** 15 Mins.

Ingredients:

- ½ cucumber
- 3-4 spring onions
- 1 carrot
- 2 duck breasts, approximately 175g each
- 1 tsp Chinese five spice
- ½ tsp black pepper
- 2 tbsp light soy sauce
- 1 tbsp honey
- 2 tbsp sesame oil
- 100g hoisin sauce
- 10-12 Chinese style pancakes

Directions:

1. Slice the carrot, cucumber and spring onions into thin strips and set aside for later.
2. Cut the duck breasts into thin strips, mix with the Chinese five spice and black pepper.
3. Pre-heat the Evolve Grill with the deep pan plate attached to 220C.
4. Add the sesame oil and heat for a minute, place the duck pieces into the pan and cook for 3-5 minutes, stirring occasionally.
5. Add the honey and soy sauce and cook for a further 2-3 minutes.
6. Pour over the hoisin sauce and cook for a further 2-3 minutes, then remove it all from the grill and set aside to a bowl (making sure it is fully cooked through).
7. Heat pancakes per package instructions, grab your chopped veg from earlier, and dig in!

Cheats Calzone Pizza

Servings: 4

Ingredients:

- Pre made or homemade pizza dough
- Tomato purée or ketchup
- 1 red onion
- Handful of grated cheese
- Additional favourite fillings such as ham, mushrooms or sweet corn

Directions:

1. Roll out the pizza dough to be slightly larger than a slice of bread.
2. Leave 1cm edge all around and spread tomato purée/ketchup sprinkle with sliced red onion, cheese and any other filling.
3. Fold in half and press the dough together with a fork. If desired, put a little butter on the dough for an extra crispy finish when it cooks.
4. Pre-heat your George Foreman Grill until ready.
5. Place the pizza on the grill and cook for up to 10 mins or until it is ready.
6. Also works well with pre bought puff pastry, or even a slice of normal bread.

Notes:

1. when placing the folded pizza base on the George Foreman Grill, make sure you place the folded edge at lower part of the grill so you don't lose any of the tasty filling. For an authentic pizza flavour, use buffalo mozzarella and fresh basil. This recipe also works well with puff pastry or even a slice of normal bread.

George Foreman Grilled Shishito Peppers

👥 Servings: 2

Ingredients:

- Shishito peppers
- Oil
- Salt and pepper

Directions:

1. Toss the shishitos in a bit of oil, salt, and pepper
2. Grill on the George Foreman for ~2 minutes or until skins are a little browned and flesh is cooked through
3. If desired, add a splash of seasoning like balsamic vinegar or soy sauce

Lentil Dahl

👥 Servings: 2-4   🕐 Cooking Time: 20 Mins.

Ingredients:

- 1 tbsp sunflower oil
- 1 medium white onion, finely chopped
- 1 garlic clove, finely chopped
- ½ tsp ground coriander
- ½ tsp ground cumin
- ½ tsp turmeric
- ¼ tsp cayenne pepper
- Pinch of salt and pepper
- 100g butternut squash, diced into 1cm sized chunks
- 450ml vegetable stock
- ½ tin chopped tomatoes
- 120g red lentils
- ½ bunch fresh coriander, chopped
- To serve:
- 70g rice per person, cooked per package instructions
- Naan bread
- Pappadums
- Mango chutney

Directions:

1. Pre-heat your George Foreman Evolve Grill with the deep pan attached to 1750, then add the sunflower oil and heat through.
2. Add the onion and garlic, and cook for 3-5 minutes until the onions are soft but translucent.
3. Stir in the ground coriander, cumin, turmeric, cayenne pepper, salt, pepper and butternut squash, and cook off the spices for a few minutes, stirring regularly so they don't burn.
4. Add the stock and chopped tomatoes, then bring to the boil.
5. Once boiling, reduce the heat and simmer for approximately 10 minutes, stirring occasionally so nothing sticks or burns.
6. Stir in the lentils and simmer for a further 20 minutes or so, stirring every now and again until the lentils and butternut squash are soft and fully cooked.
7. Finally, stir through the coriander and serve with your choice of rice, pappadums, naan and a dollop of mango chutney!

Notes:

1. if you prefer sweet potato, feel free to substitute for the butternut squash - just follow the recipe as per the normal instructions!

POULTRY RECIPES

Grilled Greek Chicken Kabobs With Tzatziki Sauce

Servings: 6

Ingredients:

- 6-inch wooden skewers
- MARINADE:
- 2 lbs. chicken breasts cut into 12 strips
- 2 tbsp olive oil
- 1 tsp dried mint
- 2 tbsp plain yogurt
- Salt and pepper to taste
- 2 tbsp red wine vinegar
- 2 tbsp minced garlic
- 2 tsp dried oregano
- TZATZIKI SAUCE:
- ½ cucumber
- 1 tsp dillweed
- 1 tbsp lemon juice
- 1 tsp minced garlic
- 1 tbsp olive oil
- ½ cup plain yogurt

Directions:

1. In a large bowl add olive oil, yogurt, vinegar, garlic, oregano, mint, salt, and pepper. Mix together to combine.
2. Add chicken to marinade, toss to coat. Cover and place in the refrigerator for at least 2 hours.
3. Make the tzatziki sauce: Peel the cucumber and use a spoon to scoop out all the seeds. Finely dice the cucumber and add it to the bowl. Add yogurt, lemon juice, olive oil, dillweed, garlic and salt and pepper to taste. Mix until fully combined. Cover and refrigerate at least 20 minutes or overnight.
4. About an hour before grilling, soak the wooden skewers in water. Thread the strips of chicken onto the skewers.
5. Preheat the your GEORGE FORMAN® grill to 425°F. Once the grill is preheated, place the skewers on the grill. Cook for about 4 minutes or until a thermometer inserted in the thickest part registers 160°F or above.
6. To serve: Can eat just by dipping into the tzatziki sauce or you can pull out the skewer and make a pita sandwich with the suggested toppings.
7. Toppings, optional:
8. Pita pockets
9. Thinly sliced red onions
10. Diced tomatoes
11. Hummus

Air Fryer Homemade Chicken Tenders

 Servings: 4

Ingredients:

- ½ cup flour
- 3 tsp. salt
- 2 tsp. pepper
- 2 eggs, beaten
- 6 cups sour cream & onion potato chips, finely crushed
- 1 lb. fresh boneless, skinless chicken breast tenders
- DIPPING SAUCE
- ½ cup plain whole milk Greek yogurt
- 1 Tbsp. dried minced onion
- ½ tsp. dill weed
- ½ tsp. dried parsley
- ½ tsp. garlic salt

Directions:

1. In a shallow dish, add the flour and season with salt and pepper. In a separate shallow dish, add the beaten eggs. In a final shallow dish add the crushed chips.
2. Working in batches, coat chicken tenders in the flour, then egg and finally in the chips. Coat both sides of chicken well in chips. Place on a large cutting board and repeat with remaining chicken.
3. Place baking rack in the bowl in the high position and place 4 chicken tenders on top.
4. Tap the bake button and set temperature to 400°F and fry for 10 minutes, flipping halfway through. Repeat with remaining chicken.
5. Meanwhile, in a small bowl, stir together all dipping sauce ingredients. Cover and place in refrigerator until ready.
6. Serve chicken tenders hot with dipping sauce.

George Foreman Grill Chicken Quesadillas

 Servings: 2   Cooking Time: 5 Mins.

Ingredients:

- 2 Large flour tortillas 1 tortilla per quesadilla
- 1 teaspoon chopped cilantro
- 1/2 cup shredded Monterey Jack cheese or shredded
- Taco cheese
- 1/2 cup diced tomatoes
- 1/3 cup fresh sliced green onions

Directions:

1. Layout tortilla flat and add cheese to just 1/2 of it. On top of cheese add tomatoes, cilantro, grilled chicken and green onions.
2. Fold other half of tortilla over cheese half and brush a little vegetable oil on both sides.
3. Add to preheated Foreman Grill (use medium setting) and close lid. Check after 2 minutes for doneness. Quesadillas will be ready in 2-5 minutes.

Notes:

1. The possibilities are endless! If you like black beans, here is a nice quesadilla for you.

George Foreman Grill Lemon Garlic Chicken

Servings: 4

Ingredients:

- 1/4 cup fresh lemon juice (about 1 lemon)
- 1/4 cup olive oil
- 3 cloves garlic, minced
- 1/8 teaspoon kosher salt, or to taste
- 1/8 teaspoon ground black pepper, or to taste
- 1 pound boneless, skinless chicken breasts (about 4 large fillets)

Directions:

1. Gather the ingredients.
2. In a large bowl, whisk together lemon juice, olive oil, garlic, salt, and pepper.
3. Add the chicken breasts, turning to coat with the marinade. Refrigerate and let marinate chicken for 30 minutes.
4. Preheat the grill. Cook chicken breasts on the grill 5 to 6 minutes or until cooked through. If using a regular grill, turn chicken breasts halfway through the cooking time.
5. Transfer to plates and serve immediately.
6. Preparation Tips: Using the George Foreman Grill to Make Chicken
7. There are a few simple things to keep in mind when grilling chicken with the George Foreman grill.
8. For tender results, use only boneless chicken breasts or thighs. The meat can be cooked as is or pounded with a meat tenderizer for faster cooking.
9. Chicken must always be cooked until thoroughly done (about 4 to 6 minutes) to make sure you don't get sick. Don't cut into the chicken halfway through cooking on the George Foreman grill — the juices will run out and you'll end up with a dry piece of chicken.
10. To check if fully cooked through, touch the center of the breast with a fork to note firmness. The cooked chicken breast should feel firm, but not hard. Alternatively, you can use a meat thermometer to check the internal temperature; it should be at least 165 F.

Notes:

1. Cleanup Tips: Immediately after you are done grilling your chicken, unplug the grill and spritz the grilling surfaces with water. When the grilling surfaces have cooled, wipe the grill plates using mild dish soap on a moist sponge or paper towel. Using a clean paper towel with a spritz of water, wipe the grill clean.

Lemon Tarragon Chicken With Grilled Zucchini And Potatoes

Servings: 2

Ingredients:

- 2 6-oz boneless skinless chicken breasts
- 1 12-oz bottle lemon tarragon dressing (Recommended: Briannas)
- Fresh tarragon leaves for garnish
- Lemon slices for garnish
- FOR THE POTATOES:
- 1 large baking potato, scrubbed and dry
- 2 Tbsp olive oil
- 1 tsp salt
- ½ tsp ground black pepper
- ½ tsp granulated garlic
- FOR THE ZUCCHINI:
- 1 zucchini, cut into rounds (discard the ends)
- 2 Tbsp olive oil
- 1 tsp salt
- ½ tsp black pepper
- 1 tsp Italian Herb blend or any combination of herbs that you like

Directions:

1. For the chicken: Put the chicken in a gallon-sized food storage bag and pour enough dressing over the chicken to cover it. There will be leftover dressing; you can use it as a sauce once the chicken is done. Put the chicken in the refrigerator to marinate for at least 30 minutes up to 2 hours.
2. For the potatoes: While the chicken is marinating, take the potato and slice it into half-inch-thick rounds, discarding the ends and leaving the skin on. Depending on the size of the potato you should get 6-8 rounds. In a gallon-sized food storage bag, combine the oil, salt, pepper, and granulated garlic. Add in the potato slices and toss until they are evenly coated with the oil mixture. Set aside until ready to cook.
3. For the zucchini: In a gallon-sized food storage bag, combine the olive oil, salt, pepper, and Italian Herb blend. Add in the zucchini slices and toss until they are evenly coated with the oil mixture. Set aside until ready to cook.
4. When ready to cook, preheat the grill to 400°F and preheat your oven to 170°F. You can't cook all of this at once on the grill so you'll need the oven to keep the food warm.
5. Once the grill is preheated, place the chicken breasts on the grill and close the lid. Cook the chicken until a thermometer inserted into the thickest part reaches 165°F, about 12-15 minutes. Move the chicken from the grill to a plate, cover with aluminum foil, and place in the warm oven until ready to serve.
6. Place the potato rounds on the grill and close the lid. Cook the potatoes until they are crispy on the outside and soft in the center, about 18-20 minutes. You can test with a knife by inserting it in the potato and seeing how easily the potato slides off. If it slides off quickly the potato is done, but if it sticks to the knife it is not. Once the potatoes are done, place them on the plate with the chicken in the oven while you cook the vegetables.
7. Place the zucchini slices onto the grill and close the lid. Cook the zucchini until tender crisp, about 5 minutes. Once the zucchini is done, pull the plate from the oven. Transfer one of the chicken breasts and half of the potatoes to another plate and then divide the zucchini evenly between the two plates. Turn off the grill and unplug it.
8. If desired, drizzle some dressing over the chicken and garnish with the lemon slices and fresh tarragon sprigs. Serve immediately.

Stuffed Chicken Breast

Servings: 2 **Cooking Time:** 26 Mins.

Ingredients:

- 1 lb chicken breast
- 4 oz. cream cheese, softened
- ½ cup baby spinach, chopped
- ½ cup cherry tomatoes, sliced
- 2 Tbsp. shaved parmesan cheese
- 1 tsp. dried basil
- ⅛ tsp. dried oregano
- ½ tsp. minced garlic
- Salt and pepper to taste

Directions:

1. In a medium bowl mix together the cream cheese, spinach, cherry tomatoes, Parmesan, basil, oregano, garlic and salt and pepper.
2. Cut a long horizontal slit through the thickest side of the chicken breast, nearly to the other side, to create a pocket for the filling, being careful to cut all the way through. Season each side of the chicken breast with salt and pepper.
3. Fill each pocket with half of the cream cheese mixture. Use toothpicks, if necessary, to hold the pocket closed.
4. Preheat the Indoor|Outdoor grill on Setting Place the stuffed chicken breasts on the preheated grill. Place the lid on the grill.
5. Grill the chicken breasts for 14 minutes on one side. Carefully flip the chicken and continue grilling, with the lid on, for 12 more minutes. Let the chicken rest for 5 minutes before serving.

Best Damn George Foreman Grill Chicken Breasts

Servings: 2 **Cooking Time:** 10 Mins.

Ingredients:

- 2 boneless, skinless chicken breasts, 6-8oz each, 1/2" thick
- 2 tsp dried oregano
- 1 tsp onion powder
- 1 tsp paprika
- 1/2 tsp garlic powder
- 1/2 teaspoon kosher salt
- 1/2 teaspoon ground black pepper
- 2 tsp olive oil

Directions:

1. Preheat your grill with the lid closed for at least 5 minutes or until it indicates hot.
2. If necessary, pound chicken breasts to 1/2" thick or slice in half horizontally.
3. Add olive oil to chicken. Mix dry ingredients and rub onto chicken.
4. Add seasoned chicken to preheated grill, close lid, and grill 4-6 minutes or until internal temperature reaches 165°(F). Give the chicken a turn halfway through cooking to get the nice crisscrossed grill marks.
5. Let rest for 2 minutes before enjoying.

Jerk Chicken Thighs

Servings: 6

Ingredients:

- 2 lbs. bone-in, skin on, chicken thighs
- ½ tsp. ground cumin
- ⅛ tsp. cayenne
- 2 tsp. allspice
- ½ tsp. cinnamon
- ¼ tsp. cardamom
- 2 Tbsp. dark brown sugar
- 1 tsp. salt
- ½ tsp. pepper

Directions:

1. Attach upper and lower grill plates and preheat Grill & Broil to 400°F.
2. In small bowl, mix together all spices and season both sides of chicken thighs with mixture.
3. Place chicken thighs on preheated grill and grill for 15-17 minutes, or until chicken reaches internal temperature of 170°F.
4. Remove from grill and allow thighs to rest for about 5 minutes before slicing and serving.

Pesto And Parmesan Chicken Wings

Servings: 8

Ingredients:

- 4 lb. chicken wings, separated and tips removed
- 2 Tbsp. lemon juice
- 1 tsp. finely grated lemon zest
- 2 Tbsp. olive oil
- 1/4 cup grated parmesan cheese
- 1/2 cup prepared pesto

Directions:

1. Preheat grill on setting #4. In a large bowl, stir together pesto, olive oil, lemon juice and zest. Toss with chicken wings until coated.
2. Grill, covered and turning as needed, for 20 to 25 minutes or until cooked through. Arrange chicken wings on a platter; sprinkle with Parmesan cheese.
3. Tip: Add a pinch of hot pepper flakes to the pesto mixture for chicken wings with some bite.

Notes:

1. For a zesty dip, serve the chicken wings with a blue cheese dipping sauce.

Parmesan Lemon Chicken Recipe

Servings: 4

Ingredients:

- 1 ½ lbs. boneless, skinless chicken breasts or tenders
- ⅓ cup flour
- 1 cup bread crumbs
- 1 cup Parmesan cheese (grated), separated
- 1 tsp. dried parsley
- ½ tsp. salt
- ½ tsp. pepper
- 3-4 lemons
- 1 Tbsp. minced garlic
- 1 stick (½ cup) melted butter, separated
- 8 Tbsp. lemon juice
- 1 Tbsp. lemon pepper seasoning
- 3 Tbsp. olive oil
- 3 Tbsp. honey
- Optional: fresh parsley, 1 lemon for topping

Directions:

1. Preheat George Foreman Grill and Broil to 400°F.
2. Grab three bowls. Add flour to one bowl. Combine bread crumbs, ½ cup grated Parmesan cheese, dried parsley and about 1/2 teaspoon each of salt and pepper and stir. In final bowl, add 1-2 teaspoons lemon zest, 4-5 tablespoons lemon juice, minced garlic, and 5 tablespoons melted butter. Stir. Remove 4 tablespoons of this mixture and set aside.
3. Slice chicken breasts to size of tenders (about 1-inch strips) or use chicken tenders. Coat in flour, heavily dredge in garlic-lemon mixture, and then coat in Parmesan bread crumb mixture. Place on prepared sheet pan. Use any remaining Parmesan bread crumb mixture and sprinkle over tenders. Sprinkle lemon pepper seasoning over tenders.
4. Place chicken tenders on preheated grill. Grill for 8 minutes per side and flip tenders to other side.
5. Use oven mitts or hot pads to remove top grill plate and place on heat resistant surface. Sprinkle chicken tenders with remaining cheese and turn Grill & Broil to "Broil" function after removing top grill plate.
6. Allow to broil until crispy top layer forms and cheese is melted but not burnt or approximately 2 minutes. If desired, place lemon slices over chicken (optional).
7. Meanwhile, whisk remaining 3 tablespoons melted butter, 3 tablespoons lemon juice, 1-2 teaspoons lemon zest, 3 tablespoons olive oil and 3 tablespoons honey in small bowl. Add some pepper and parsley if desired.
8. Remove from grill and top with honey-lemon mixture and fresh parsley, if desired, and enjoy immediately.

Turkey Meatballs

Servings: 2-3 **Cooking Time:** 15 Mins.

Ingredients:

- 250g turkey mince
- ½ white onion, finely chopped
- 2 cloves garlic, finely minced
- 3 sprigs flat leaf parsley, finely chopped
- 100g grated cheddar cheese
- ½ tsp cayenne pepper
- ½ tsp ground mace
- ½ tsp paprika
- Salt to taste

Directions:

1. Mix all ingredients together, form into balls no more than 2cm in height. Cover and refrigerate for 20 minutes.
2. Pre-heat the Evolve Grill with the deep pan plate attached to the maximum temperature.
3. Add 1 tbsp. of oil and add the meatballs, close the lid and cook for 5 minutes, open lid and move the meatballs around, close the lid and cook for a further 5 minutes. Repeat this again and check the meatballs are cooked through.
4. Serve with a tomato pasta sauce and spaghetti of your choice, and top with grated parmesan.

Chicken Quesadillas

Servings: 8

Ingredients:

- 1 teaspoon vegetable oil
- 1 1/2 cup chopped green bell pepper
- 1 cup minced red onion
- 2 teaspoons ground cumin
- 2 cups cooked chicken breast
- 1 can (14.5 ounce size) diced tomatoes, drained
- 1/4 cup minced fresh cilantro
- 1/4 teaspoon salt
- 1/4 teaspoon ground black pepper
- 8 flour tortillas (8-inch size)
- 3/4 cup shredded Monterey jack cheese

Directions:

1. Heat the oil in a large skillet over medium-high heat. Add the bell pepper and onion. Cook, stirring frequently, for 3-4 minutes or until the onion is soft.
2. Stir in the cumin, cooked chicken, and diced tomato. Cook, stirring frequently, for 3 minutes. Add the cilantro, salt, and pepper.
3. To assemble the quesadillas, place about 1/2 cup of the chicken mixture on one half of each tortilla. Sprinkle with the cheese. Fold the tortilla in half and press lightly.
4. Heat a ungreased nonstick skillet over medium heat. Add the quesadillas in batches and cook until browned on one side. Carefully flip the quesadillas over and cook on the other side until browned and the cheese is melted. Repeat with remaining filled tortillas.
5. Serve with salsa and/or sour cream for dipping.
6. This can also be made in a sandwich grill or other contact grill.

Buffalo Ranch Chicken Sliders

Servings: 8

Ingredients:

- 1 cup buffalo hot sauce
- 1.5 lbs. chicken breast
- ⅓ cup mayonnaise
- 2 Tbsp. milk
- 1 packet dry ranch dressing mix, divided
- 8 slider buns
- 2 Tbsp. sour cream

Directions:

1. In a medium bowl, mix together the hot sauce and 2 Tbsp of the dry ranch dressing mix.
2. Cut the chicken into eight, 2" chunks and toss in the hot sauce mixture. Cover the bowl with plastic wrap and refrigerate for at least an hour, or overnight.
3. Preheat the Indoor/Outdoor grill on setting 4.
4. Place the chicken on the preheated grill. Place the lid on the grill.
5. Grill the chicken for 6-8 minutes a side.
6. Meanwhile, in a small bowl, mix together the remaining dry ranch dressing mix, mayonnaise, sour cream and milk to create a dressing.
7. Top one bun with a chicken slider and a drizzle of ranch dressing. Serve warm.

Piri Piri Chicken

Servings: 4   **Cooking Time: 20 Mins.**

Ingredients:

- 1 whole medium chicken, cut up into breast, wings, thighs, drumsticks
- For the piri piri sauce–
- 4 large red chillies,
- 3 cloves garlic, finely chopped
- 1 tsp paprika
- 1 tsp oregano
- 50ml red wine vinegar
- 100ml olive oil

Directions:

1. For the piri-piri sauce, roast the chillies for 10-12 minutes, chop and add to a pan with all the other ingredients. Simmer for 2-3 minutes then leave to cool slightly and blend with a hand mixer or in a food processor.
2. Rub the piri-piri sauce over all the chicken pieces, then cover with cling film and refrigerate for at least 20 minutes to marinate, or overnight for a deeper flavour if you have time.
3. Pre-heat your favourite George Foreman Grill to maximum and cook the chicken in batches of pieces that are of a similar size for 10-15 minutes until cooked through and the juices run clear.
4. Serve with your favourite sides and dig in – we recommend chunky chips and a side salad for treat you'll happily get messy for!

Creamy Cheesy Chicken Parcels

Servings: 2   **Cooking Time:** 20 Mins.

Ingredients:

- 1 lean chicken breast with skin removed
- 75g-100g reduced fat cream cheese
- 100g fresh baby spinach leaves washed & dried
- 1 tsp mustard powder
- 1 tsp grated nutmeg
- 1 tsp pepper
- 2 flour tortilla wraps

Directions:

1. Pre-heat your favourite George Foreman Grill to maximum, then add on the dry spinach leaves; cook for around 20–30 seconds until wilted, then remove and squeeze out any excess moisture by wringing them out in a clean tea towel.
2. Season your chicken breast with salt and pepper and grill for 6-8 minutes. Once cooked all the way through, remove and cut into strips.
3. In a bowl, mix your chicken strips into the cream cheese, mustard powder, nutmeg, pepper and spinach, making sure to combine thoroughly.
4. Spoon your creamy chicken mixture onto the centre of each tortilla wrap, fold in each end and roll up.
5. Place seam side down on a hot grill and heat for 2 minutes until warmed.

Korean Chicken Thighs

Servings: 3-6   **Cooking Time:** 15 Mins.

Ingredients:

- 6 chicken thighs, boneless and skinless
- 1 tsp toasted sesame seeds
- 2 spring onions, thinly sliced
- For the marinade:
- 3 large cloves garlic, minced
- 5g fresh ginger, minced
- ½ tbsp Gochujang chilli paste or chilli paste
- 90g dark brown sugar
- 1 tsp sesame oil
- 1 tbsp honey
- 60ml dark soy sauce
- 1 tbsp rice wine vinegar
- 2 tsp corn flour
- 1 tbsp cold water

Directions:

1. Make a marinade by adding the garlic, ginger, chilli paste, brown sugar, sesame oil, honey, soy sauce, and wine vinegar to a saucepan, and bringing it to a boil. Once boiling, reduce the heat to a simmer.
2. Meanwhile, whisk together the corn flour and water until well combined, then whisk into the marinade mixture. Bring to the boil once more, then remove from the heat to completely cool.
3. Taking 2 long skewers, skewer the chicken thighs, making sure that each thigh has both skewers going through it. Brush the cooled marinade over the chicken thighs and refrigerate for 20-30 minutes.
4. Pre-heat your favourite George Foreman Grill, place the chicken thigh skewer on the grill and cook for 8-12 minutes or until cooked through and the juices run clear.
5. Sprinkle with the toasted sesame seeds and spring onions and serve straight away!
6. We recommend pairing with a crispy fried egg and veggie fried rice for the perfect mid-week treat!

Yorkshire Pudding Wrap

Servings: 2   **Cooking Time:** 10 Mins.

Ingredients:

- 2 giant Yorkshire puddings
- 1 large chicken breast, roasted, sliced
- 4 rashers smoked streaky bacon, cooked
- 4 chipolata sausages, cooked
- 150-200g ready-made stuffing
- 1 small carrot, cooked, sliced
- 6-8 green beans, cooked
- Few spoons of gravy for each

Directions:

1. Pre-heat your favourite George Foreman Grill to maximum.
2. Lay the giant Yorkshire puddings on a plate or chopping board and layer up the stuffing, carrots and peas, bacon, sausage and the roast chicken in the middle. Top with gravy.
3. Fold in the edges to make a wrap and grill with the seam-side down so it doesn't unravel.
4. Cook your Yorkshire pudding until it is crispy on the outside and piping hot in the middle, this will depend on how well stuffed your Yorkshire pudding is! Serve immediately and enjoy!

Chicken Wings

Servings: 4-6   **Cooking Time:** 15 Mins.

Ingredients:

- 12 chicken wings or thighs or a mix
- For the marinade -
- 200ml tomato ketchup
- 2 tbsp honey
- 1 tbsp soy sauce
- 2 tbsp chilli sauce
- 1 tbsp chilli powder
- 3 cloves garlic, crushed
- Salt and pepper

Directions:

1. Combine all the ingredients for the marinade and mix well.
2. Pour over the chicken and mix well.
3. Pre heat the grill to maximum. Cook the chicken on both sides until cooked through and the juices run clear.

Filipino Grilled Chicken

Servings: 4   **Cooking Time:** 30 Mins.

Ingredients:

- 720ml water
- 240ml apple cider vinegar
- 120ml fresh lemon juice
- 120ml soy sauce
- 2 Tbsp. minced garlic
- 2 Tbsp. sugar
- 1 Tbsp. crushed red pepper
- 1 Tbsp. black peppercorns
- 5 bay leaves
- 4 chicken breasts (either whole or cut into halves)
- rapeseed oil, for brushing
- salt and pepper, to taste

Directions:

1. In large, sturdy resealable plastic bag, combine all ingredients except oil, salt and pepper. Seal bag and shake to evenly distribute marinade over chicken.
2. Open bag and press out air; re-seal and refrigerate overnight.
3. Remove chicken from marinade. Pat chicken dry and let stand at room temperature for approximately 30 minutes.
4. Meanwhile, preheat Indoor/Outdoor Grill to setting
5. Brush chicken with oil and season with salt and pepper.
6. Place chicken on grill and cook, turning occasionally, until lightly charred after about 30 minutes.
7. Transfer chicken to platter and let rest for 10 minutes before serving.

Chicken Kebabs

Servings: 2-4   **Cooking Time:** 15 Mins.

Ingredients:

- 3 chicken breasts, skinless and boneless
- 2 tbsp tandoori paste
- 1 lemon juice
- 2 cloves garlic, finely crushed
- 1 small courgette
- 1 white onion

Directions:

1. Firstly, soak your wooden skewers in water for 30 minutes so they don't burn once on the grill.
2. In a bowl, combine the tandoori paste, lemon juice and garlic, then set aside.
3. Dice the chicken evenly into cubes approximately 1-2 cm in size, and add to the tandoori mixture.
4. Separately, dice the courgette and onion into similar sized pieces as your chicken.
5. Thread your marinated chicken, courgette and onion onto skewers, alternating throughout.
6. Place your skewers onto a large plate, cover and leave in the fridge to marinate for at least 20 minutes, or overnight if you're making these in advance.
7. Pre-heat your favourite George Foreman Grill to maximum; place the kebabs onto the grill, shut the lid and cook for 8-12 minutes until cooked through and the juices run clear.

SNACKS AND APPETIZERS RECIPES

Sweet Potato Hash Browns With Bacon

Servings: 2-4   **Cooking Time:** 15 Mins.

Ingredients:

- 8-12 rashers streaky bacon
- For the hash browns -
- 2 medium sweet potatoes
- ½ white onion, finely sliced
- 1 ½ cloves garlic, finely chopped
- 70g corn flour
- 2 tbsp olive oil plus extra for cooking
- Salt and pepper to taste
- To serve -
- 4 spring onions, finely sliced
- 150-200ml sour cream

Directions:

1. Start by peeling and grating the sweet potatoes, then rinse well with cold water. Drain and squeeze any excess water out of the potatoes using a clean tea towel or a fine cloth, then transfer the potato to a bowl.
2. Mix in all other ingredients, then divide the mixture into about 8 equal amounts, and shape into balls.
3. Pre-heat your favourite George Foreman Grill, and cook your sweet potato hash browns in batches for 8-12 minutes until crispy and golden brown on the outside.
4. Remove has browns from the grill and cook the bacon for 6-8 minutes.
5. To serve, layer the hash browns with 3-4 rashers of bacon, then top with some soured cream and sprinkle with spring onions; dig in and enjoy!

Bbq Pulled Jackfruit

Servings: 2-4   Cooking Time: 15 Mins.

Ingredients:

- For the BBQ Sauce:
- ½ white onion, finely chopped
- 1 clove garlic, finely chopped
- 60g tomato ketchup
- 10ml dark soy sauce
- 1 tbsp dark brown sugar
- 1 tbsp vegan Worcestershire sauce
- ½ tbsp malt vinegar
- 3-4 drops tabasco sauce
- ¼ tsp mustard powder
- For the filling:
- 2 tbsp olive oil
- 2 x 565g tins of jackfruit in brine or water
- 2 tbsp olive oil
- 1 onion, finely diced
- 2 cloves garlic, finely chopped

Directions:

1. Drain the jackfruit and cut the root parts off, set aside.
2. For the BBQ sauce, attach the deep pan plate to your George Foreman Evolve Grill and pre-heat to 2200 Add the oil and heat for 1 minute. Add the onion and garlic and cook for 3-4 minutes, stirring occasionally. Carefully add the tomato ketchup, dark soy sauce, dark brown sugar, vegan Worcestershire sauce, malt vinegar, tabasco sauce and mustard powder, and mix well. Cook for 4-5 minutes, stirring occasionally. Once cooked, turn the grill off and allow the sauce to cool. Remove into a bowl and set aside for later.
3. Clean your deep pan plate, reattach and reheat to 2200 Add the oil and heat for 1-2 minutes.
4. Add the onion and garlic, cook for 2-3 minutes until soft. Add the jackfruit and cook for 5-6 minutes, stirring occasionally. Stir in the BBQ sauce and cook for a further 2-3 minutes. Pull apart the jackfruit using a fork until it is all shredded, and remove from the grill.
5. Serve at your next BBQ in your favourite burger bun with slaw or salad for a delicious vegetarian/vegan treat!

Air Fryer Tortilla Chips

Servings: 8

Ingredients:
- 12 small fajita tortillas
- 2 Tbsp. olive oil
- 2 tsp. chili powder
- 1 tsp. paprika
- 1 tsp. cinnamon
- 2 tsp. onion powder
- 2 tsp. garlic powder
- 1 tsp. salt
- ½ tsp. pepper

Directions:
1. Cut the tortillas into 8 triangles and place in a large bowl. Add oil and toss to coat.
2. In a small bowl, mix together chili powder, paprika, cinnamon, onion and garlic powders, salt and pepper.
3. Pour half of the seasoning mix over the tortillas and toss to coat. Repeat with the remaining seasoning.
4. Place 1/2 of the tortillas in the drum and fit the lid on top. Insert into the bowl.
5. Tap the air fry button and set temperature to 350°F and fry for 15 minutes.
6. Remove and spread in an even layer on a baking sheet. Repeat with remaining seasoned tortillas.
7. Enjoy with your favorite salsa or guacamole.

Roasted Pumpkin Salad

Servings: 2-4   **Cooking Time: 20 Mins.**

Ingredients:

- ½ pumpkin, deseeded and cut into wedges
- 2 red onions, peeled and cut into wedges
- 4 tbsp olive oil
- Leaves of 3 sprigs of thyme
- Salt and pepper
- 1 block feta cheese, cut into chunks
- 100g pomegranate seeds
- 80g pumpkin seeds, roasted
- 80g pine nuts, roasted
- 250g pre-cooked quinoa
- Honey and balsamic dressing
- Rocket leaves

Directions:

1. Brush the pumpkin and onion wedges with olive oil, season with salt and pepper, and sprinkle with the thyme leaves.
2. Pre-heat your favourite George Foreman Grill to maximum. Grill the pumpkin and onion wedges for 4-8 minutes until pumpkin is soft in the middle and charred on the outside. Once cooked, remove from the grill and set aside.
3. To serve, season the quinoa with salt and pepper and any remaining thyme if you'd like. Spoon onto a serving plate, then arrange the rocket leaves, pumpkin, onion and feta cheese on top. Sprinkle with the pomegranate, pumpkin seeds, and pine nuts, and then drizzle with the dressing. This dish works perfectly as a BBQ side or a dinner party starter, and any leftovers work great for lunches!

Courgette Feta Fritters With Tzatziki

Servings: 2-4   Cooking Time: 10 Mins.

Ingredients:

- 4-5 medium courgettes approx. 650-700g
- 1 tsp salt
- ½ white onion, finely diced
- 40g plain flour
- 40g parmesan cheese, finely grated
- 2 cloves garlic, finely chopped
- 100g feta cheese, crumbled
- 1 large free range egg
- Salt and pepper to taste
- For the tzatziki –
- 250g Greek yoghurt
- 1 cucumber
- 3 cloves garlic, finely diced
- 1 tsp lemon juice
- 1 tsp chopped fresh mint
- 1 tbsp olive oil
- Salt and pepper to taste

Directions:

1. To make the tzatziki, deseed the cucumber and dice into small chunks approximately ½cm big. Add to a bowl along with the Greek yoghurt, 3 cloves of the garlic, lemon juice, mint, and olive oil. Season with salt and pepper to taste, mix well and set aside.
2. For the courgette fritters, grate the courgettes and mix with the salt, place in colander and leave for 10 minutes.
3. Using a clean kitchen towel, squeeze all of the liquid out of the courgette. Transfer into a large bowl and mix with the onion, flour, parmesan, garlic, feta cheese, egg and seasoning to taste.
4. Divide the mixture into equal amounts and shape into burger-like patties.
5. Pre-heat your favourite George Foreman Grill, and cook the courgette fritters in batches for 6-9 minutes with the lid closed, checking occasionally to make sure they don't burn. You want to cook them until they are lightly browned and crispy on the outside with nice defined char marks.
6. Serve with the tzatziki.

George Foreman Whole Roasted Brussel Sprout Stalk

Servings: 10

Ingredients:
- stalk Whole brussel sprout
- 1/2 cup oil
- 1 tsp salt
- 1 tsp pepper

Directions:
1. Rinse the whole brussel sprout stalk in cold water, and a make a little foil boat for it out that goes about 1/3 of the way up the sides.
2. Combine the oil, salt, and pepper in a bowl and use a brush or your hands to fully and thoroughly coat the brussel sprouts and stalk
3. Roast at 420° for 50 minutes, turning once after 30 minutes. We used a pellet grill, but the oven will do just fine. It should be a little browned all around, and you should be able to easily slide a fork through the brussels.
4. To serve, give each person a sharp steak knife. The individual guests can stab the sprouts with their fork with one hand and cut them off with the other. I served it with a Betty Crocker pot roast recipe, greek yogurt mashed potatoes, pan drippings gravy, and a dark red wine. Some people like to make a honey mustard or cheese sauce to dip them in. It would make a very impressive vegetarian turkey substitute or vegan turkey substitute for Thanksgiving, if that's something you're into.
5. There will be leftovers, so cut off the sprouts and freeze them in quart bags
6. Cut the stalk into a few pieces and add it to a crock pot with water on low to make vegetable stock overnight.
7. The stock is roasty and rich and complex and delicious. We used it to make shiritake ramen and minestrone noodle casserole
8. Another suggested shaving the stalk and using the bits as an artichoke substitute. The shaved bits of the stalk turn out like, well, any other 'boiled to death' vegetable shavings that have been turned into stock. They are edible, sure, but not not very delicious. I figured that if I wanted to make brussel cheese dip, I'd use the plenty of tasty leftover sprouts I had in the freezer.
9. I did try the vegan bone marrow thing, and it was an interesting novelty, but it tasted bitter and chalky and overcooked and awful. I managed to choke one down because well, might as well try everything once...
10. To perfectly reheat the brussel sprouts, grill the frozen sprouts for 7 minutes until hot throughout.

Mexican Bean Chilli

Servings: 2   **Cooking Time:** 20 Mins.

Ingredients:

- 1 tbsp olive oil
- 1 onion, finely diced
- 2 cloves garlic, finely chopped
- ½ red chilli, finely chopped
- 1 tbsp tomato puree
- 1 tsp ground cumin
- 1 tsp smoked paprika
- 1 tsp chilli powder
- Pinch of salt and pepper
- 1 x 400g tin of chopped tomatoes
- 1 x 400g tin mixed beans
- 1 x small tin of sweetcorn
- Top tip: you can swap out the fresh chilli for ½ tsp of dried chilli flakes if you don't have it!

Directions:

1. Pre-heat your George Foreman Evolve Grill to 190°C with the deep pan plate attached.
2. To the deep pan plate, add the oil, onions, garlic and fresh chili, and cook for 4-5 minutes stirring occasionally.
3. Once the onions have become translucent and cooked through, add the tomato puree, cumin, paprika, chilli powder, salt and pepper, and cook for a further 2-3 minutes, stirring occasionally.
4. Add in the chopped tomatoes, drained sweetcorn and drained mixed beans and give a good mix through. Cook for a further 10-15 minutes until the mixture is fully heated and the beans are nice and tender.
5. Serve with your choice of rice and top with a spoonful of soured cream and guacamole as desired - dig in and enjoy!

George Foreman Roasted Hatch Green Chile

Servings: 2

Ingredients:

- 1-2 lbs fresh green chiles. (Hatch, Anaheim, or Pueblo)

Directions:

1. Grill the whole green chiles for 5-10 minutes, until they are blistered and cooked fully through.
2. Steam the grilled chiles in a plastic bag, a tupperware, or a covered bowl for 15 minutes. DO NOT SKIP
3. Peel the skin off

Easy Grilled Green Beans

Servings: 2   **Cooking Time: 4 Mins.**

Ingredients:

- 1/2 lb green beans
- 1-1/2 TBS extra virgin olive oil (EVOO)
- Sea salt and freshly ground pepper to taste

Directions:

1. Place the beans in a colander and rinse well under cold running water. Dry the beans by placing them on paper towels and blotting with another towel. Trim the stem ends of the beans while the grill returns to high heat. Place the beans in a large bowl, add the EVOO, and toss to coat.
2. Grill the beans in batches for approximately 3 to 6 minutes until slightly tender. They can remain a bit crisp. Place the beans on a serving platter and season with salt and pepper to taste.
3. Optional: You can squeeze some fresh lemon juice over the cooked beans or drizzle some balsamic vinegar on top.

VEGETABLES RECIPES

Chilli Grilled Sweet Potato

⏲ Cooking Time: 15 Mins.

Ingredients:

- 2 sweet potatoes
- 3 tbsp olive oil
- Salt and pepper to taste
- For the dressing:
- 3 red chillies, roughly chopped
- ½ bunch fresh coriander, finely chopped
- ½ bunch fresh parsley, finely chopped
- 1 shallot, finely diced
- 1 clove garlic, finely chopped
- 150ml olive oil

Directions:

1. For the dressing, add the chillies, garlic and shallot to a pan with the olive oil. Heat the contents of the pan to just before it starts to sizzle and remove from heat and leave to cool.
2. Drain the ingredients from the oil and finely chop. Return the ingredients to the oil along with the finely chopped herbs and mix well, season and set aside. This can be made in advance.
3. For the sweet potatoes, pre heat your favourite George Foreman grill.
4. Peel and slice the potatoes into thick disks. Brush with the olive oil and season.
5. Place the potato disks on the grill, shut the lid, and cook for 10-15 minutes or until soft.
6. Once the potatoes are cooked, place on a plate and spoon the dressing over and serve.

Mexican Corn

👥 Servings: 5

Ingredients:

- 5 half ears of sweet corn, shucked
- 2 Tbsp butter, melted
- 4 Tbsp mayonnaise
- ½ tsp garlic powder
- ½ tsp chili powder
- ½ cup cotija cheese, crumbled (or sub parmesan cheese)
- 3 Tbsp cilantro, chopped
- 1 lime

Directions:

1. Preheat the Indoor/Outdoor grill on setting 5.
2. In a small bowl, combine the mayonnaise, garlic powder and chili powder; set aside.
3. Brush the ears of corn with the melted butter and place onto the preheated grill. Place the lid on the grill. Grill for 15 minutes, turning throughout to cook on all sides.
4. When the corn is done, brush with the mayonnaise mixture and sprinkle with the cotija cheese and cilantro.
5. Squeeze the lime juice on top of the corn and serve warm.

Waffled Mashes Potatoes

Servings: 8

Ingredients:

- 3 large baking potatoes, peeled and chopped
- 2 Tbsp. butter, melted
- ⅓ cup milk
- 2 eggs
- ½ cup flour
- 1 tsp. baking powder
- 1 tsp. garlic powder
- 1 tsp. onion powder
- 1 tsp. salt
- ½ tsp. pepper
- ¼ cup chopped chives
- 1 cup shredded cheddar cheese

Directions:

1. In large stockpot, add chopped potatoes and fill with just enough water to cover potatoes.
2. Bring water to boil over medium-high heat and boil for 8-10 minutes, or until potatoes are soft enough to pierce with fork.
3. Drain potatoes and place back on burner. Turn down heat to low and cover for 15 minutes.
4. Attach upper and lower waffle plates and preheat Grill & Broil to 425°F.
5. In large bowl, mash potatoes with hand masher until smooth.
6. Mix in remaining ingredients until combined. Add additional milk if mixture seems too thick.
7. Scoop ½ cup of mixture into center of each waffle plate. Close lid and cook for 7-8 minutes, or until waffles are crisp.
8. Remove waffles and place on wire rack to cool. Repeat with remaining mixture.

Stuffed Mushrooms

Servings: 6   **Cooking Time:** 10 Mins.

Ingredients:
- 12 (1-2 inch diameter) white mushrooms, stems removed
- 25g parmesan cheese
- 25g chopped green olives
- 25g black olives, pitted
- 25g minced red onion
- 1 garlic clove, minced
- 1 tbsp mayonnaise

Directions:
1. Preheat the Evolve Grill to 180°C degrees with the deep pan attached. Lightly pull the stems off the mushrooms – this should make enough room for the filling, if not, hollow out slightly with a spoon.
2. Mince the mushroom stems and mix together with the remaining ingredients.
3. Spoon 1tsp of filling into each mushroom.
4. Place the stuffed mushrooms on the grill. Cook for 5 to 6 minutes until the cheese is melted and the mushrooms are cooked through.

Notes:
1. To clean mushrooms, wipe caps with a dry paper towel.

Air Fryer Honey Garlic Cauliflower Bites

Servings: 4

Ingredients:

- 2 (10 oz) bags cauliflower florets
- 2 Tbsp. olive oil
- 4 Tbsp. low sodium soy sauce
- 1 tsp. sesame oil
- 2 tsp. apple cider vinegar
- 4 Tbsp. honey
- 1 ½ Tbsp. minced garlic
- ½ tsp. salt
- ¼ tsp. pepper

Directions:

1. In a large bowl, whisk together the oil, soy sauce, sesame oil, apple cider vinegar, honey, minced garlic, salt and pepper.
2. Add the cauliflower florets and toss to coat.
3. Place the cauliflower florets in the drum and fit the lid on top. Insert into the bowl.
4. Tap the air fry button and set temperature to 425°F and fry for 30 minutes.
5. Serve as a crunchy appetizer, or with rice and your favorite cooked protein.

Basic Grilled Crimini Mushrooms Recipe

Servings: 2   **Cooking Time:** 5 Mins.

Ingredients:

- 1 lb small crimini mushrooms*, or baby bellas
- 2 TBS extra virgin olive oil (EVOO)
- 1/2 tsp sea salt
- 1/2 tsp freshly ground black pepper
- *Button mushrooms will also work for this recipe.

Directions:

1. Clean the mushrooms by wiping off any dirt with a damp paper towel. Trim the stems down to be even with the mushroom caps. While the grill returns to high heat, place the mushrooms in a large bowl, add the EVOO, and toss to coat. Sprinkle with the salt and pepper and toss once more.
2. Grill the mushrooms stem side down with the top closed for 4 to 5 minutes until they get nice grill marks.

Grilled Broccoli For A Pan Or Outdoor Grill

 Servings: 4

Ingredients:
- 4 tablespoons olive oil, divided
- 2 tablespoons freshly squeezed lemon juice
- 1 teaspoon garlic powder, or finely minced garlic
- Freshly ground black pepper, to taste
- 5 to 6 cups broccoli florets
- 1/2 cup grated Parmesan cheese
- Sea salt, to taste

Directions:
1. Place 3 tablespoons of the olive oil in a large mixing bowl. Add the lemon juice, garlic powder, and pepper. Whisk until combined.
2. Add the broccoli to the marinade, tossing with your hands to coat well. Let stand at room temperature for 15 to 20 minutes. Just before cooking, drizzle the remaining tablespoon of olive oil over the broccoli, and toss to coat well.
3. Preheat your indoor contact grill. Or, if using a grill pan, preheat over medium-high heat.
4. Grill the broccoli until tender when pierced with a fork, about 10 minutes, if using a contact grill, or 15 to 20 minutes if using a cast-iron pan or grill. Turn it as it browns so that all of the sides get caramelized. Transfer the broccoli to a serving bowl. Sprinkle with most of the Parmesan cheese, and season with salt to taste. Toss, give another sprinkle of Parmesan on the top and serve immediately.

Vegan Chickpea Curry

Servings: 2   **Cooking Time:** 20 Mins.

Ingredients:
- 1 tbsp vegetable oil
- 1 red onion, finely chopped
- 1 garlic clove, finely chopped
- ½ red chilli, chopped
- 2 tomatoes, chopped
- 2 tbsp mild curry paste
- 1 x 400g tin chopped tomatoes
- 2 x 400g cans chickpeas, drained and rinsed
- 250g bag baby leaf spinach
- ½ bunch fresh coriander, chopped
- ½ lemon, juice
- 1 large naan
- 4 onion bhajis
- Optional extras:
- Basmati rice, cooked to pack instructions
- Mango chutney

Directions:
1. Heat the oil in a saucepan then add the onions and cook for 2-3 minutes. Stir in the garlic and chilli and add a lid for 3-4 minutes until the onions have softened, making sure to stir occasionally so nothing sticks or burns.
2. Mix in the curry paste and cook for a further 4-5 minutes, then add the tomatoes and cook for 4-5 minutes. Add the chickpeas and close the lid to bubble away for a further 8-10 minutes.
3. While the curry is cooking, turn on your grill and add your onion bhajis. Grill for 4 minutes or until piping hot and starting to crisp. Remove from the grill and cook the naan for 3-4 minutes.
4. Turn off the heat on your curry and stir in the spinach, coriander, and lemon juice and mix thoroughly.
5. Serve with the grilled naan and bhajis, alongside basmati rice and mango chutney for a delicious Indian-inspired meal!

Easy Foil Potatoes

Servings: 4

Ingredients:
- GARLIC POTATO
- 1 lb. new potatoes
- 1 small onion, sliced
- 1 Tbsp olive oil
- 1 tsp. garlic powder
- 1 tsp. onion powder
- ½ tsp. salt
- ¼ tsp. pepper
- 1 Tbsp butter
- RANCH POTATO
- 1 lb. new potatoes
- 1 Tbsp olive oil
- 2 Tbsp dry ranch dressing mix
- 1 Tbsp butter

Directions:
1. Wash and scrub potatoes clean; dry and cut larger potatoes in half.
2. Place the garlic potatoes and onion in one zip top bag. Place the ranch potatoes into a separate zip top bag. Pour the oil into each of the two bags and zip close.
3. Shake each bag to evenly coat the potatoes and onions in oil.
4. For the garlic potatoes, sprinkle the garlic powder, onion powder, salt and pepper into the zip top bag and shake again to evenly coat.
5. For the ranch potatoes, sprinkle the dry ranch dressing mix into the zip top bag and shake again to evenly coat.
6. Preheat the Indoor/Outdoor grill on setting 5.
7. Tear off two large pieces of aluminum foil, folding up all four sides to create a "basket" for the potatoes. Pour the potatoes into the foil "baskets".
8. Place the butter on top of the potatoes and cover with another piece of foil.
9. Place the foil packets of potatoes onto the grill. Place the lid on the grill.
10. Grill the potatoes for 30-35 minutes, until the potatoes are fork tender.

Balsamic Grilled Beet Salad

Servings: 4-6

Ingredients:

- ⅓ cup balsamic vinegar
- ¼ cup sugar-free grape jelly
- ⅓ cup olive oil
- ½ tsp. salt
- ¼ tsp. pepper
- 3 medium beets, peeled and sliced, about ⅛" thick
- ½ cup crumbled Gorgonzola
- 2 oz. pine nuts, about ½ cup*
- 5 oz. arugula
- DRESSING
- 2 Tbsp. balsamic vinegar
- 1 Tbsp. sugar-free grape jelly
- 2 Tbsp. olive oil
- 1 tsp. minced garlic
- ¼ tsp. salt
- ⅛ tsp. pepper

Directions:

1. In a medium-size bowl, whisk together vinegar, jelly, oil, salt and pepper.
2. Place sliced beets in marinade and toss to coat. Cover bowl and place in refrigerator for
3. 20 minutes to marinate.
4. Preheat George Foreman grill by plugging it in, or setting it to MAX, 400°F or setting Place marinated beets on preheated grill and close lid. Grill for 10 minutes until tender.
5. Note: if grilling on Indoor/Outdoor grill, grill for 5 minutes per side.
6. Meanwhile, assemble salad. In large bowl, toss together arugula, Gorgonzola and pine nuts.
7. Add cooked beets and toss to combine.
8. In a small bowl, whisk together dressing ingredients. Drizzle over salad and toss to coat.
9. Enjoy as a side salad or add favorite cooked protein.

Roasted Corn Salsa

Servings: 8

Ingredients:

- ¼ cup apple cider vinegar
- 6 slices bacon, cooked and crumbled
- ¼ cup chopped cilantro, loosely packed
- 2 green onions, thinly sliced
- 2 tsp. honey
- 2 Tbsp. diced red onion
- 4 ears, fresh sweet corn, kernels removed from cobs
- ½ cup diced seedless cucumber

Directions:

1. Attach griddle plate to Grill & Broil, preheat on HIGH Broil at 350°F.
2. Brush griddle surface with small amount of oil. Add corn and broil 10 minutes, stirring halfway through cooking until corn is lightly browned.
3. Transfer corn to medium bowl. Add remaining ingredients, stir to combine.
4. Cover, refrigerate at least 30 minutes to allow flavors to blend.

Notes:

1. To save time, reheat fully-cooked bacon and cut into pieces. If fresh corn is no longer in season, substitute 2 cups of frozen corn, thawed.

Balsamic Carrots

Servings: 4

Ingredients:
- 1 lb. carrots, cleaned and cut in half
- 1 Tbsp. brown sugar
- 1 Tbsp. olive oil
- 1 Tbsp. honey
- ¼ cup balsamic vinegar
- ¼ tsp. cayenne powder
- 1 tsp. garlic powder
- ¼ tsp. pepper
- ¼ tsp. salt

Directions:
1. Place the carrots in a medium sized shallow dish. Drizzle the oil and honey over the carrots and turn to completely cover the carrots.
2. Sprinkle the garlic powder, cayenne powder, salt and pepper over the carrots, turning to coat.
3. In a small saucepan, combine the balsamic vinegar and brown sugar and bring to a boil. Reduce heat to low, allowing the mixture to thicken, until it coats the back of a spoon.
4. Pour the glaze over the carrots and toss to mix.
5. Preheat the Indoor/Outdoor grill on setting 4.
6. Place the carrots onto the grill. Place the lid on the grill.
7. Grill the carrots for 10 minutes per side, until the carrots are crisp-tender.

Grilled Stuffed Aubergine

🍽 Servings: 2-4   🕒 Cooking Time: 15 Mins.

Ingredients:

- 2 aubergines
- 1 white onion, finely chopped
- 2 cloves garlic, minced
- ½ red chilli, finely chopped
- 200g feta cheese
- Pomegranate seeds
- ½ bunch flat leaf parsley, finely chopped
- 4 tbsp olive oil
- Salt and pepper to taste
- For the dressing -
- 60g tahini paste
- 55ml Greek yoghurt
- ½ lemon juice
- 2 cloves garlic, minced
- 85ml water
- 70ml olive oil
- Salt and pepper to taste

Directions:

1. For the dressing, combine the tahini, Greek yoghurt, lemon juice, garlic, water, 70ml olive oil, salt and pepper in a small bowl and set aside.
2. Slice each aubergine in half lengthways and scoop out the middle onto a chopping board – be careful not to puncture the skins when doing this, as you'll want them in one piece later on!
3. Roughly chop the fleshy part of the aubergine that you removed from the skin, and set aside.
4. Heat half of the remaining olive oil in a frying pan and cook the onion, garlic and chilli until soft and golden brown, then add the chopped aubergine from earlier and cook for a further 6-8 minutes, stirring at regularly.
5. Pre-heat your Grill & Melt Grill to maximum with the grill plates attached. Brush the remaining olive oil over the aubergine skins and season.
6. Grill for 3-4 minutes then carefully remove and turn off the grill to cool. Fill your aubergine skins with the cooked aubergine and onion mixture, then top with some crumbled feta, making sure not to overfill too much!
7. Once cooled to the touch, remove the top grill plate to activate the melt function, and turn the grill back on. One up to temperature, place the stuffed aubergines back onto the grill, close the lid and cook for a final 2-4 minutes.
8. Remove from the grill and drizzle over some of the dressing, then finish with some pomegranate seeds and chopped parsley.
9. Serve alongside a leafy salad or your favourite seasonal vegetables for a delicious healthy meal!

Spinach And Ricotta Lasagne

Servings: 4-6   **Cooking Time:** 20 Mins.

Ingredients:
- 60g butter
- 60g plain flour
- 600ml milk
- 2 tbsp olive oil
- 750-900g spinach leaves
- 12 lasagne sheets
- 500g ricotta cheese
- 100-150g parmesan cheese, finely grated
- Salt and pepper

Directions:
1. In a hot pan on the hob, heat the oil and cook the spinach in batches until it is all wilted. Leave to cool on kitchen paper and set aside. Once fully cooled, squeeze as much water out of the spinach as you can, and set aside.
2. To make the béchamel sauce, start by melting the butter in a non-stick saucepan on a medium-low heat. Once fully melted, add the flour and mix to fully combine, forming a roux (you might find it easier to do this with a whisk, but a wooden spoon will work too). Keep stirring the roux on the heat for a further 30 seconds to ensure the flour is cooked through. Then, gradually stir or whisk in the milk making sure it is fully combined - do not add the milk all at once or your béchamel sauce will be lumpy. You may not need all of the milk, so keep an eye on the consistency as you're going along.
3. To assemble your lasagne, firstly grease the bottom of your Evolve deep pan plate, then spread over a little béchamel sauce followed by a layer of 4 lasagne sheets. Spread a little more béchamel on top of your lasagne sheets then top with half of the drained the spinach and half of the ricotta. Top with a further layer of 4 lasagne sheets. Repeat this using the remaining spinach and ricotta cheese. Save some béchamel for the top. On the final layer of lasagne sheets top with the remaining béchamel and sprinkle with the parmesan.
4. Attach the deep pan plate to your grill, cover the top with a piece of baking paper and heat to 160°C. Cook for 15-25 minutes until golden brown on top and cooked all the way through.

Grilled Teriyaki Tofu

Servings: 4

Ingredients:

- 1 Tbsp. ground ginger
- 1 Tbsp. honey (or agave)
- 1 Tbsp. rice vinegar
- 2 Tbsp. sesame oil
- 3 Tbsp. low sodium soy sauce
- 15 oz. extra firm tofu

Directions:

1. Drain tofu and remove from package.
2. Cut tofu into ¾-inch slices and lay out flat between paper towels.
3. Put weighted cooking sheet on top and press tofu, for 30 minutes. (This will remove water from tofu and allow marinade to soak up.)
4. While tofu is draining, mix together soy sauce, rice vinegar, sesame oil, honey, and ground ginger in medium bowl.
5. Marinate drained tofu in mixture for at least one hour.
6. Preheat Indoor/Outdoor Grill on setting 4 and grill tofu for 3 minutes per side.
7. Remove from grill and serve immediately with rice and vegetables.

Printed in Great Britain
by Amazon